W9-BKQ-737

ALANIS
MORISSETTE

You Oughta Know YOU OUGHTA KNOW

PAUL CANTIN

Stoddart

Published in 1997 by
Stoddart Publishing Co. Limited
34 Lesmill Road
Toronto, Canada
M3B 2T6
Tel. (416) 445-3333
Fax (416) 445-5967

01   00   99   98   97   1   2   3   4   5

Stoddart Books are available for bulk purchase for sales promotions,
premiums, fundraising, and seminars. For details, contact the
Special Sales Department at the above address.

Canadian Cataloguing in Publication Data

Cantin, Paul
Alanis Morissette: you oughta know

Includes index.
ISBN 0-7737-5871-2

1. Morissette, Alanis.   2. Rock musicians - Canada - Biography.   I. Title.

ML420.M678C23 1997   782.42166'092   C97-930288-9

"Fate Stay with Me"; "Find the Right Man": copyright © by Captain Tom
Music Publishing and reprinted with permission.
Dalmy's theme song: reprinted with permission of Stephan Klovan.

Every reasonable effort has been made to contact the holders of copyright for materials
quoted in this book. The author and publisher will gladly receive information that will
enable them to rectify any inadvertent errors or omissions in subsequent editions.

Cover Design: Bill Douglas @ The Bang
Text Design: Tannice Goddard
Typesetting: Kinetics Design & Illustration

Printed and bound in Canada

*Stoddart Publishing gratefully acknowledges the support of the
Canada Council and the Ontario Arts Council in the development
of writing and publishing in Canada.*

"You should know," said Estella. *"I am what you have made me. Take all the praise, take all the blame; take all the success, take all the failure; in short, take me."*

— CHARLES DICKENS, *GREAT EXPECTATIONS*

Contents

PART TWO: YOU LEARN

Preface

A funny thing happened with my e-mail in 1996. A couple of times each month, I would receive messages from complete strangers, asking if I could share any information about Alanis Morissette's past. Sometimes the messages were flattering and polite. Sometimes they were brusque. Sometimes they came from foreign countries and were written in fractured English. Some sounded creepily obsessive. Most were earnest and straightforward. But the correspondents all seemed hungry for any crumb of insight into the singer's personality.

As a reporter with the *Ottawa Sun*, a daily newspaper in Alanis's hometown, I had spent the better part of the past year following her steep rise to the top of the charts on the strength of her album *Jagged*

Little Pill. I interviewed the singer, followed her to her victories at the Grammys and Junos, watched her perform a half-dozen concerts, and reported on each of her triumphant achievements. Some of my work had been posted on the *Sun* newspaper chain's web site, CANOE (http://www.canoe.ca), which is how the global fraternity of Alanis admirers had tracked me down.

The mail I received wasn't typical fan letter stuff, full of breathless declarations of her greatness or frantic for details about her favourite flavour of ice cream. These were sincere appeals for more information, something to help these people put her music into perspective. They were wondering where all these amazingly powerful songs were coming from.

There's something about the intimacy and honesty of Alanis's music that inspires curiosity. And that curiosity triggered this project. The whole world knows her music, but her past is shrouded in mystery, misunderstanding, rumour, and myth. I soon realized I wanted to tell Alanis's story, and in order to do it I would have to turn to her friends, associates, collaborators, and, of course, to Alanis herself.

One of the most fascinating things I discovered along the way was that Alanis found a new audience by making art not in spite of her personal problems, but out of inspiration from them. Her faith in her own artistic instincts is the real legacy of *Jagged Little Pill.* What helped her learn to trust those instincts is the crux of this book.

None of this would have been possible without the kindness of many people. The *Ottawa Sun* graciously granted me a leave of absence from my duties as rock critic and assisted me greatly with library and photographic resources. Publisher John Paton, Editor-in-Chief Rick VanSickle, Managing Editor Rob Paynter, and Today section editor Brian Gorman were never less than enthusiastic and encouraging. Likewise, the good wishes of my colleagues in the editorial department and Denis Cyr and the photography crew were much appreciated. I'm fortunate to work with great people.

This project would not have happened without the faith and prodding of two friends — Heather Bird and Tralee Pearce. John

Sakamoto, who runs Jam! Entertainment on the CANOE web site, commissioned me to prepare a multimedia feature on Alanis Morissette, and some of the research for that piece formed the backbone of this book. I value John's suggestions and friendship very much. *Toronto Sun* parliamentary bureau chief Robert Fife provided some much-needed eleventh-hour advice, as did my father-in-law, author David Williamson. And key sources (both named and unidentified) gave their time, memories, and resources to this project; I am very grateful for their cooperation and understanding.

Martha Sharpe at Stoddart coached me through the book-writing process with patience and good humour, providing encouragement and very necessary wake-up calls. And even when time was no longer on our side, my editor, Lynne Missen, expertly guided me through to the completed manuscript. I am indebted to Martha and Lynne.

My family has provided a lifetime of support and I thank them now and always. My favourite columnist, copy editor, best friend, and wife, Linda Williamson, helped me through this and other challenges and I thank her with all my heart.

Paul Cantin
Ottawa, February 1997

Prologue

The sun over Molson Park is setting, painting the sky red and orange. On the ground below, thirty-five thousand restless Alanis Morissette fans are clustered around a gargantuan empty stage, growing audibly impatient, waiting for the day-long concert's main event. Throughout the day, a parade of performers has attempted to entertain the audience, but it's clear who they're here to see.

Behind the stage rigging, amid a tangle of tents, trucks, and sound equipment and a snarl of electronic cables, is a collection of prefab buildings that serve as dressing rooms at the remote concert site, located a short drive north of Toronto near the town of Barrie. From there, you can hear the echoey thud of prerecorded music roaring through the stage PA system and the faint chirp of the first cricket, the impatient screams of admirers eager for the headliner and the gentle crunching sound of footsteps on gravel, the crackle of a backstage staffer's walkie-talkie and the whisper of gossip being exchanged among the music industry insiders milling about.

The August sky darkens, the crowd noise takes on a more anxious tone, and the action backstage moves up a notch as crew members make final preparations — hustling instruments to the stage, planting bottles of Evian water on top of amplifiers, taping set lists to the floor.

"Let's go," a voice says, and a group of five musicians, heads bowed in solemn concentration, emerges from the dressing room and begins a slow march toward the stage, four men surrounding a petite twenty-two-year-old woman, her long brown hair falling like a curtain across her features. The scene looks like something from a boxing match — a prize fighter surrounded by cornermen and trainers, making their way to the ring. But there's no bravado evident among the crew. Only a steely determination to get the job done, a focus honed from more than a year spent together on the road and, for Alanis Morissette, over a decade battling to establish herself as an entertainer and an artist.

In countless media profiles, writers have commented that she is more striking in person than in photos, and it's true. She exudes a casual, offhanded beauty. As she finds her focus, her large brown eyes are hidden, cast downward, and her prominent jaw is locked in concentration. Walking to the stage, she pulls her hair away from her high forehead, and then unexpectedly smiles brightly.

Onstage, the lights are shut off, plunging the field into darkness. A piercing, collective scream tears through the crisp evening air, high and harsh, and from the stage you can see and hear crowd members struggle to push closer to the spectacle.

A low bass note rumbles from the PA, and guitarists Nick Lashley and Jesse Tobias pluck out a vaguely Middle Eastern melody. At the back of the stage, hidden behind a thicket of percussion instruments, drummer Taylor Hawkins adds gentle accompaniment on his cymbals, before crashing in with rolling tom-tom fills. Bassist Chris Chaney joins in with jolting accents. They're off.

The moshpit at the front of the stage seethes into a whirlpool of action: crowd surfers lunge atop their neighbours, spinning and diving and wrestling in a jumble of sweat-soaked heads, flailing arms, and Doc Marten–covered feet. The music builds to a crescendo of wah-wah distorted notes. From the wings comes the wheezing sound of a harmonica, and Alanis glides onstage to join in.

The music has to be loud or it would be easily overwhelmed by the greeting she receives. Alanis bends forward and paces in an impatient circle. Her blues harp pressed to her mouth with both hands, she coaxes long, ragged chords from the instrument, seemingly oblivious to the reaction she has inspired a few yards away.

From the audience, Alanis must look confident, bold. But from up in the stage rigging, where her parents, Alan and Georgia, are watching, she seems frighteningly small before the intimidating sea of faces. And yet there is no hesitation as the introduction ends and the ensemble shifts without pause into "All I Really Want," a wish list of the singer's most cherished desires.

Above the din of the music and the ecstatic crowd, Alanis confides her dearest wish to find a single soul mate, hitting on the real irony at the centre of her newfound fame and acceptance.

By articulating the dark, lonely frustrations of her life, Alanis Morissette has connected with the thousands on this field and millions more around the world. Her quest to find a single soul mate has linked her to a generation (or generations) of alienated souls.

▽

Where once it seemed no one in the Canadian music business cared about her, on this day, more people have turned up to see her in concert than paid to see the summer's other two big Molson Park shows — a Neil Young/Oasis double bill (thirty thousand people), and the day-long alternative extravaganza, Lollapalooza (twenty thousand).

Two years ago, with two albums of dance-pop to her name, Alanis was living alone in nearby Toronto, mending a broken heart and trying to become a serious songwriter and singer, but unable to shake her reputation as a teen star, Canada's answer to Tiffany. She was considered a has-been by the time she was old enough to vote. The Canadian music scene, which is heavily centralized in Toronto, dismissed her as a joke. With few willing to take her seriously and even fewer willing to take a chance on releasing a third album, she relocated to Los Angeles and created the songs that would become *Jagged Little Pill*.

Alternately indignant and tender, *Jagged Little Pill* has become a worldwide phenomenon; fans everywhere, especially young women, have been drawn to Alanis's whimsical observations and scathing indictments, buying her music in record-shattering quantities. She dominated the 1996 Grammy awards, graced the covers of both *Rolling Stone* and *Spin*, and toppled all the competition for chart sales. Between September 1995 and August 1996, Alanis was off the MTV and VH1 video charts for a mere week. By 1997, *Jagged Little Pill* had sold twenty-six million copies worldwide, and counting. Industry sources have predicted it could go on to become the third biggest selling album in U.S. history, behind Michael Jackson's *Thriller* and The Eagles' *Their Greatest Hits*.

While other touring acts struggled to fill venues in the summer of 1996, Morissette's Can't Not tour was a roaring success, racking up rave reviews, winning her thousands more fans, and, according to the concert industry publication *Pollstar*, grossing over $23 million — making her one of the year's top touring acts.

While the triumphs and accolades have been plentiful, a skeptical and vocal minority took exception to her transformation and has opted out of the coronation ceremonies, branding her success a calculated, cunning bit of image manipulation. She bombed as a dance queen, so she restyled herself as an alternative chick — so goes the cynical theory.

But even as her face became a fixture in magazines and on music video programs and her voice rang from radios around the world, fans and detractors have wondered: "Who *is* Alanis Morissette?" Some have suggested she has attempted to hide her past; others have pointed out that the honesty and brutality of much of *Jagged Little Pill* is wholly informed by those early experiences. Whatever image critics and fans have tried to pin on her, the simple fact is she is nothing more or less than the sum total of a remarkable life.

Yet for someone who seemingly grew up onstage with a bright smile glued to her face, much of the anguish and effort that went into the making of *Jagged Little Pill* took place away from the public eye. To fully understand the voice behind songs like "You Oughta Know," "You Learn," "Perfect," and "Hand in My Pocket," we have to go right back to the beginning.

One

FATE STAY WITH ME

*"I would not change a thing.
I am really happy with who I have
become and the space I am in now.
I know every link in the chain had
something to do with it."*
— ALANIS MORISSETTE

1

Starting Early

Alanis Morissette's determination and self-assurance can largely be traced to her parents, particularly her mother Georgia, whose own childhood was marked by a harrowing journey to Canada.

Georgia Feuerstein arrived in Canada as a child from her birthplace in Hungary, having escaped the 1956 anti-Soviet uprising. She was only ten years old when her family fled by train in November, 1956. Their escape was nearly foiled when their train was stopped and searched by Soviet forces. A sympathetic conductor warned the family and had the engineer unleash a cloud of steam, which let the Feuersteins slip off the train in the smoke and confusion. When it later pulled away, the family could see from a distant hiding spot that their fellow escapees had been forced off the train at gunpoint.

Later, in exchange for whatever worldly possessions they had carried with them — watches, jewellery, money — a farmer let them travel at night across his land to the Austrian border. As they made their way to the frontier, search flares were sent up in an attempt to spot escapees. The family had to dive for cover to escape detection.

A month later, Georgia and her family arrived in Canada and initially lived at the Uplands military barracks in Ottawa. At the time, Georgia's knowledge of English consisted of little more than "yes" and "no." When fire drill alarms rang out at school, she assumed it was a bomb-attack warning and instinctively cowered under her desk.

Georgia met Alan Morissette in a schoolyard when she was twelve years old, and they became sweethearts. Georgia's strict European parents did not allow her to date, and so they spent their time together playing badminton, broomball, and street hockey. Alan also tutored her in the French language. Later that summer, he announced she would one day be his wife.

Nine years later, he delivered on that promise. They married in the summer of 1967 in Ottawa, during a long weekend break from their summer courses at Queen's University in Kingston, Ontario.

After graduating, the Morissettes moved back to Ottawa. Their first child, Chad, arrived in 1971, and three years later, on June 1, 1974, Georgia gave birth to twins at the Riverside Hospital in Ottawa. Alanis was born twelve minutes after her brother, Wade. Alan wanted his daughter to have a female variation on his own name and nearly settled on Alana, until he spotted a reference to the more distinctive Alanis in a book about Greece.

Georgia and Alan now found themselves the parents of three children, and they settled down to provide for their young family. Like many first-generation immigrants, Georgia has a relentless work ethic. For eighteen years, she was a school teacher and has also worked intermittently at everything from selling Fuller brushes door to door, to marketing air and water filters, home alarms, and utility audits. Where Georgia is gregarious, outgoing, and exuberant, Alan, a high school principal, is described by friends as reserved and academic. The couple may seem like a study in contrasts, but Alanis's personality naturally bridges the two. In conversation, Alanis takes after her father and can come across as analytical and quiet. Yet onstage, she is perfectly comfortable holding the attention of thousands, and, like Georgia, she has a tireless drive to achieve.

In 1977, Alan and Georgia accepted positions teaching the children of Canadian servicemen stationed in Lahr, Germany, at one of Canada's primary NATO bases in Europe. Almost every weekend during their time overseas, the Morissettes took their children travelling across Europe in a camper-van, visiting Holland, Austria, Germany, Yugoslavia, Greece, Switzerland, and France. Alanis was bright, talkative, and active, and even at three, she was drawn to the spotlight. During the family's trek to the French city of Avignon, Alan took her to see Olivia Newton-John's 1977 cinematic debut in *Grease*. Alanis was so taken with the movie, she quickly committed the songs and storyline to memory. When her maternal grandmother later came to visit them, Alanis performed the entire film, using a nail polish bottle as a microphone. "As parents, you say 'cutsie, cutsie,'" Georgia told the *Ottawa Citizen* in 1987. "But by God, she had the words down pat."

In 1980, the Morissettes returned to Ottawa, where they have lived ever since. Alanis's recent fame has brought new attention to the city, whose limelight is usually focused on the prime minister and elected officials who make up the federal government. Ottawa became the capital of Canada largely because it represented a compromise, falling as it does right on the border between Canada's two cultural solitudes, English Ontario and French Quebec, and Canada's two largest cities, Toronto and Montreal. For many, Ottawa still represents a compromise. Often damned with the faint praise of being "a nice place to raise kids," it is also occasionally derided as the city that fun forgot.

In a sense, Ottawa is a company town like many others. But in this case, the company is the federal bureaucracy. With so many citizens employed in the civil service, making reasonably similar amounts of money and having so much in common, many have looked at Ottawa and seen a largely homogeneous population. And compared to other major cities in Canada, that may be true. The uniformity of salaries continually ranks Ottawa at or near the country's highest average income bracket.

Most of the famous people associated with Ottawa are, naturally, politicians. Residents often have the modest thrill of seeing the prime minister or cabinet members climbing out of limos en route to the nation's business. But even before Alanis's success with *Jagged Little Pill*, some of Canada's biggest musical and entertainment exports called Ottawa home. Bryan Adams grew up in a military family and hopscotched around the world throughout his childhood, but it was while living in Ottawa's Beacon Hill neighbourhood that he bought his first guitar and joined his first band — an incident later immortalized in his song, "Summer of '69."

In the late fifties, a local teen named Paul Anka recorded a song about his unrequited love for his babysitter, and "Diana" became one of the biggest hits of the early rock 'n' roll era. Then in 1974 — the year Alanis was born — he returned to the top with "You're Having My Baby," a treacly tribute to his wife's fecundity.

Ottawa-bred impressionist Rich Little has a street named after him. Actor Dan Aykroyd, who began his dramatic career in campus productions at Ottawa's Carleton University, and *Saturday Night Live* cast members Norm McDonald and Mark McKinney all lived in the city at one point. For a brief time, a youngster named Tommy Mapother lived in Ottawa with his mom and sisters, and would later become better known as actor Tom Cruise. U.S.-based news anchor Peter Jennings and *Friends* star Matthew Perry lived and worked in Ottawa, too.

In the late sixties and early seventies, the city became a hub for the burgeoning folk movement, and the nightspot Le Hibou became a major stop on the coffeehouse circuit. The most celebrated and enduring product of that scene is the politically committed and still active singer, songwriter, and guitarist Bruce Cockburn. And in 1971, Ottawa's Five Man Electrical Band scored a continental hit with the hippie protest anthem "Signs."

When they settled back in Ottawa, Georgia and Alan began to foster in their three children a positive, outgoing nature, coupled with a sensitivity to their own feelings and an openness about sharing. The Morissettes attended Catholic mass every Sunday, and every night, the family gathered together to share their personal thoughts and observations of the day. To make their children feel special, Alan and Georgia would individually devote a day or evening to one-on-one activities with each child — whether it was seeing a movie or playing catch or going shopping.

All three kids showed an early interest in performing, even choreographing and videotaping dance routines to hit songs of the day, like Queen's "Another One Bites the Dust." They also acted out scenes from TV shows and movies. Gradually, Chad became more interested in other things, and eventually pursued a career in business. Wade excelled at sports and also enjoyed singing and dancing with his sister, but he wasn't as driven as Alanis, whose primary interest was always in art and entertainment. Her earliest childhood memories centre on her infatuation with show business, and she was fascinated with movies, performances, and music, wanting to take part in them herself.

Despite their diverging interests, all three Morissette kids displayed the same discipline. Whatever activity they pursued, they did it with vigour. "All three children have an attitude that says 'I'm going to do this until I reach my goal, not until the first obstacle gets in my way,'" Georgia told a TV documentary crew from Ottawa-based Carleton Productions in 1991, just as her daughter's star was on the ascent in Canada.

And Alanis wasted no time in getting started on her own goals. When she was six years old, the Morissettes arranged to visit entertainers Lindsay and Jacqui Morgan, family friends who performed as a folk duo in Ontario and Quebec in the 1970s and 1980s. The couple was booked to perform in the lounge of a hotel in the cottage region of Muskoka. Because the Morgans were performing in a licensed bar, the Morissette kids weren't allowed to go in, so the family perched on the resort's deck and watched their friends play through a set of French doors.

The performance had a profound effect on Alanis. Straining to see her friends singing onstage, she was rivetted by the spectacle and did not take her eyes off the Morgans' show. "When she looked up on that stage and saw me singing, her eyes were like saucers," says Jacqui. "She wanted to be there. I knew she was going to be there."

Alanis still recalls that night, and suspects that seeing close friends entertaining made the whole idea of performing seem like a very attainable goal. "A lot of people that age are just as capable of doing it as I was," Alanis says now. "But they may watch Carole King, and Carole King may not be a friend of the family. Whereas, with the Morgans doing it and being my parents' best friends at the time, I thought it was something I could do."

So Alanis settled on a career as an entertainer before she had even entered the double-digit age bracket. She relished any opportunity to perform, and Alan and Georgia did whatever was necessary to help her achieve her dream. If she wanted to dance, they signed her up for dance classes. If she was interested in theatre, they took her to auditions. Contrary to the cliché of the stage mother, Georgia never goaded her daughter into anything. Alanis stated her ambitions, and her parents became tireless facilitators of those dreams — providing unconditional support and encouragement.

"I realize how much freedom they gave me," Alanis says about her parents. "I also knew it was something I was destined to do. Not that I was destined to achieve some sort of external success with it, but to do it. To create. To perform."

Between the ages of nine and thirteen, Alanis participated in group jazz recitals at dance schools in Ottawa, and when she was eleven, she played an orphan in a local production of *Annie*. "But I loved music first and foremost," Alanis says. "There was a certain release and excitement that I got by being onstage. When I was younger, I saw music more from the performance end of it. To make people in the audience smile and take them away from reality."

Throughout that time, Alanis also began sitting alone up in her room, composing poems. It wasn't long before she was converting her rudimentary stabs at poetry into lyrics and setting them to melodies. Soon she was writing songs, although she kept them to herself.

In 1983 the Morissette family travelled to California, visiting the beach-side celebrity colony, Malibu. Alanis, who was nine at the time, purchased a map of superstar mansions and set out to track down the home of her heroine, Olivia Newton-John. When she found it, she marched up to the entrance, buzzed the intercom, and, with an uncanny confidence that would characterize much of her early career, spoke clearly into it: "Olivia? I don't know if you can see me. But if you can, I'm going to be big like you someday."

Alanis was already working on something that would launch her into a recording career. In early 1984, the nine-year-old mailed an audiocassette to Jacqui and Lindsay Morgan, who were living on a farm north of Toronto at the time. One side of the cassette featured songs Alanis had recorded from the radio (including Madonna's "Material Girl"). The other began with Alanis declaring: "This is another one of my favourite songs. I wrote this." And she proceeded to belt out an original composition.

The Morgans were a bit surprised to find the cassette in their mail, and even more surprised at how good it was. "I remember sitting there and thinking, there is something really special here," Lindsay Morgan says. "I could hear lyrics in there. The song was all over the place. It was like there was no structure. But she had all the music and was just singing away with no instruments."

Alanis is not certain what possessed her to send off the sample of her songs, but suspects she was interested in getting feedback from an experienced singer and songwriter. "When I first started writing songs, I wasn't even sure I had the voice to do it. So I was more into writing really horrible poems. And then I started just writing songs with music and lyrics and I put them on tape. And that's the tape I sent Lindsay."

Within a few months Lindsay was back in Ottawa and stopped by the Morissettes' house. He sat down at the family piano and asked Alanis to work with him on her song. She brought out the lyrics and music for a number she called "Fate Stay with Me," and the two painstakingly went through the rudimentary words and melody, with Lindsay pointing out trouble spots and arranging the unstudied music.

He coached her through the song, playing various chord sequences and suggesting different words, but let Alanis make all the decisions until they had a completed song.

Lindsay hung onto the musical ideas when he returned to his farm, and during spare moments, used his synthesizers, drum machines, and eight-track home recording studio to work up an instrumental backing track for the song. The next time the Morissettes came to visit, he waited until Alan and Georgia were away on an errand and sneaked Alanis into his studio to add her voice. When her parents returned, Lindsay surprised them with the finished recording. They were overwhelmed by the sound of their daughter performing her composition. Georgia burst into tears as she listened to the lyrics.

> *What did you think I'd be doing now*
> *While you left me, I was thinking aloud*
> *Would there be no end to my sorrow*
> *Will I make it through tomorrow*
> *Let the autumn leaves fall*
> *The chilly raindrops freeze*
> *The white snow melt*
> *I'll just sail on those seas.*
> *Fate, fate, fate stay with me*
> *I wanna be, wanna be, wanna be free.*

Alan and Georgia couldn't believe their young daughter had written the song. Lindsay made a copy and gave it to them. He also played it for friends, who were all astounded that a nine-year-old had written it. But Lindsay was unsure whether "Fate Stay with Me" was a fluke or whether it was evidence of real musical talent. He told Alanis to keep writing and keep him posted on her progress.

A few months later on his next pass through Ottawa, Lindsay once again took up position at the Morissette family piano and asked Alanis if she had been following his advice and working on her songs. She responded by producing an exercise book, with page after page jammed with song ideas she had worked up in her bedroom. He asked Alanis to sing one of her new songs for him.

"Now, don't laugh," she warned.

"Alanis, I am not going to laugh at all. Trust me," Morgan replied.

With that, she launched into an a cappella performance of a song called "Find the Right Man."

You find the right man in the wrong place
Once in a while, you meet him face to face
If it's love at first sight, honey you gotta fight for his love . . .
Will all this hidden emotion give you the notion
To make the first move . . .
You know you can take his heart away
Just look straight in his eyes and then you say
Can't you just see, we'll be great, you and me?

As she warbled the words, he was struck by the alarming incongruity: here was a nine-year-old brashly dispensing advice to the lovelorn, in song. And the song was pretty good. "I tell you right now, at that point, I felt the hairs on the back of my neck go up. I swear, I knew there was something really special," he says, still sounding awed.

"Find the Right Man" was so accomplished, it didn't require any polishing or embellishment from Lindsay, and it was by no means the end of her talent. Her scrapbook proved to be a treasure chest of ideas and promising song fragments. According to publishing records, two other registered songs date from that era: an Alanis solo composition entitled "I Gotta Go," and a collaboration with Lindsay called "Another Sleepless Night."

A hand-written song list prepared by a young Alanis includes those titles and "Over Now," "Get with It," "Toughen Up," "This Feeling," "Be There as My Friend," and "Your Dreams Come in Time."

Lindsay realized that "Fate Stay with Me" was no fluke; Alanis had legitimate talent and needed to go on to the next level.

"Alanis, where are you getting all this material?" he asked.

She looked at him with a twinkle in her eye and replied: "Well, it's not from experience."

Obviously, Alanis was simply taking in the sounds and techniques and vocabulary she heard on records and reinterpreting them for her own use. "She is like a sponge," Lindsay says. "When she was nine, she used to listen to Madonna. I remember one time she came up to the farm, and she was listening to (experimental Canadian songwriter) Jane Siberry. She would say: 'This is very different.' And I would play her Moody Blues. We were introducing music to each other. This nine-year-old girl talking to this old guy."

Alanis now compares her early songwriting attempts to fiction writing. She may not have experienced a broken heart, but she could imagine what one must feel like. "I think it was partly creative writing, just what I thought, writing a story — a story I might not have had any experience in."

Lindsay's enthusiasm for Alanis's budding songwriting talent encouraged Alan and Georgia to help Alanis pursue her dream of making a real record. The family agreed Lindsay was the obvious person to guide Alanis through the music business. He had experience. He had connections. He had a recording studio. And as a family friend, he had the Morissettes' trust.

In October 1985, Lindsay stood in the arrivals area at Toronto's commuter Island Airport, as a steady stream of businessmen and women climbed out of a flight from Ottawa. There, amidst the suits, was his protegée, a tall girl with short dark hair, brimming with confidence and eager to start on a new adventure — a recording career.

The pair then drove to his farm to begin work on a proper tape and promotional package, designed to impress the Foundation To Assist Canadian Talent On Record, known within the music business as FACTOR. The organization is funded by the music industry and annually hands out grants to Canadian musicians to help finance independent recordings and videos. Any money FACTOR could give Alanis would go towards producing a more polished recording, something a major record label might be interested in signing.

Lindsay was amazed at Alanis's drive. "She was just totally tireless. She worked hours and hours to perfect something." The two recorded Alanis's lead vocals and then worked out harmonies to embellish her performance. During the long hours, they also had the chance to talk, and Alanis confided to Lindsay an incident that exemplifies the kind of difficulties the young performer would soon face on a regular basis. She told him how a school friendship had gone sour after Alanis repeatedly beat out another girl at auditions. The friend said she couldn't pal around with Alanis anymore because Alanis was "too good."

"Wow, how do you feel about that?" Lindsay asked.

Alanis replied: "I can't do anything about that. How can I be less than what I am?"

In addition to recording, Lindsay also arranged a photo shoot, and had Alanis's hair and makeup specially prepared for the session. Jacqui lent her a sequined stage blouse, one of several costumes used during the session.

As the photographer snapped away, Alanis vogued, leapfrogged over a bar stool, and posed for rolls of portrait shots where she alternated silly faces with solemn, pensive looks. The camera caught her as she propped herself against a chair, demurely brandished a Japanese parasol and a fan, propped her foot on a suitcase, was frozen in a mid-air leap, and played air guitar.

Immediately after the shoot, the Morgans put Alanis on a flight back home to Ottawa. When her daughter stepped off the plane in full makeup and fashionably styled hair, Georgia was alarmed. Alanis had begun the journey as a ten-year-old, but was returning home with the look of a young woman.

But Georgia and Alan trusted Lindsay completely. He packaged up the tape with the photos and shipped it off to FACTOR, where a committee would evaluate its potential and decide whether to award them a grant. Some weeks later, the organization responded with a $3,000 cheque to kickstart Alanis Morissette's recording career.

2

On Stage and
on the Tube

As Lindsay Morgan worked on advancing Alanis's recording career, Alanis kept her eyes open for any opportunity to scratch her itch to perform.

She got her chance when her school received a visit from Dominic D'Arcy, known across Ottawa by his stage monicker, The Singing Policeman. A folk singer who entered police work in 1965, D'Arcy carved himself a unique niche in the force — and in Ottawa entertainment circles — by using his talent to deliver a positive, follow-your-dream message, delivered in school gymnasiums, hospitals, and retirement homes throughout the region. As part of his act, he would often invite talented children he had discovered along the way to perform with him.

One morning in 1985, D'Arcy had just finished his upbeat hootenanny-cum-pep-rally act at Holy Family Catholic School when the assembled students rose up and saluted him in song. As he glanced around the roomful of smiling faces singing his own patriotic anthem, "My Canada," D'Arcy's eyes fell upon one particular girl. Based on nothing more than the girl's pretty smile and enthusiastic delivery of his song, D'Arcy made a snap decision: he had to meet her. He walked over to the queue of exiting children, requested the girl step out of line, and asked her name.

"I'm Alanis Morissette," the girl answered.

"Do you sing on your own?" D'Arcy asked.

"Yes."

While they were speaking, Georgia Morissette, who was volunteering at the school, spotted the singer's interest in her daughter and invited D'Arcy back to their house for lunch. The family was interested in the advice and assistance of any experienced showbiz hand. Despite its legacy of performers and entertainers, Ottawa was not at that time exactly teeming with fast-track artists. But D'Arcy was well-known in the city and was generous with his time. Alanis also hoped that he might be interested in bringing her along as an added attraction at his shows.

After lunch, she played D'Arcy her tape of "Fate Stay with Me," and he was so impressed, he took Alanis back with him for the afternoon assembly at Holy Family and had her perform the song before a room full of her peers.

So began her association with The Singing Policeman, which would extend over two years and see them performing — sometimes with her brother Wade, who still dabbled in singing — for every conceivable community group across the Capital region. As well as her own songs and the national anthem, Alanis's repertoire included kiddie favourites like "Bingo the Dog."

"I would introduce her, saying: 'This young lady is Alanis Morissette. Remember that name, people. Her name is Alanis Morissette. She is going to be famous some day,'" D'Arcy remembers.

He once brought Alanis along to a hospital staff show, where they had their work as feel-good performers cut out for them. "These people have just come from the O.R., where a child just died," he advised Alanis. "So it is up to you and me as entertainers to spread our happiness and try to cheer these people up."

In seniors' homes, they would sometimes be confronted with an audience of slumped residents and would have to work hard to raise their spirits. "It was intense," says Alanis. "We just went anywhere. I would do these shows at $25 a pop and I'd do my two or three songs and then I'd go home. But it was fun."

Just as with Lindsay Morgan, Alanis wasn't shy about presenting her own songs and working with an adult composer. But D'Arcy's musical roots — "Irish-country," he calls them — didn't mesh with Alanis's Madonna-esque sound. He even sold Alanis his small keyboard, but the two could never find common ground when it came to composing. But as she was to demonstrate later in life, Alanis was eager to write songs with anyone who showed an interest and could provide advice and guidance.

D'Arcy did more than just provide the opportunity for on-the-job training as a performer. He preached to his pint-sized entertainer the same message he delivered to his audiences: Believe in yourself and you can do anything. D'Arcy's showbiz tutoring simply reinforced the ambition and drive to perfection Alanis already embodied.

"I've seen star quality in many, many people. But they give up," he says. "Nobody forced Alanis. We just helped her along. Her parents, the best stage parents in the world, just took her along. You want to go to the next level? We'll help you."

D'Arcy saw himself as the springboard for the children who performed with him. He taught them the basics and the values of life in show business and what it meant to give, to be responsible, to work hard, to practise. He encouraged Alanis to observe established stars like Madonna and watch not only how they perform, but also how they carried themselves offstage and mingled with the public. "If you have a dream, you have to focus. Picture yourself up there. This is all the old positive thinking, Norman Vincent Peale thing, and so on. But picture yourself doing what successful people are doing. It worked for Alanis."

He also taught her the first lesson in the art of schmoozing: learning how to take a compliment. Rather than coming across blasé or bashful, D'Arcy told Alanis to look her admirer in the eye and express her appreciation for the admiration. "If they are going to be in the world of entertainment, these are the things they have to learn," he says.

$$\triangledown$$

While D'Arcy's gigs gave Alanis exposure and experience locally, she was soon performing before an international audience as a cast member of an offbeat kids' TV show, filmed in Ottawa.

You Can't Do That on Television was a curious phenomenon. It started as a program on local TV station CJOH, but was eventually sold to the upstart U.S. cable network Nickelodeon. There, the show's irreverent version of slapstick humour and preteen energy made it an instant hit. The storyline was simply the broadly comic, madcap adventures of a group of children trying to put on a TV show.

"It was a very silly kind of program," says Abby Hagyard, who played Mom on the series. "I think in every show, the point was to give kids something that was just fun. It wasn't heavy satire, it didn't teach anything. There was no moralizing."

Because the program was targeted at preteens, cast members who matured during summer breaks were often not invited to return, and auditions for new kids were frequently necessary. Every cast was a mix of core members, who returned year after year, and a supply of new faces to replace kids who had outgrown the show. When the program first started, small classified ads in the local papers would bring out hundreds of hopeful children eager for a spot in the cast. But by the time Nickelodeon and the Canadian-based YTV network picked it up, cast members were international stars. Teen pinup magazines profiled them. They went on promotional trips to the United States (including the annual Easter egg hunt on the White House lawn, during the Reagan administration). And in the hit film *Fatal Attraction*, Michael

Douglas's daughter is even seen giggling at the show's slimings — the ritual dousing of a character with sticky green goo — a slapstick punishment applied in response to infractions like overuse of the phrase "I dunno" in response to questions from adults.

By the time Alanis auditioned (sometime in 1985), *You Can't Do That on Television* was a well-established, star-making program with obvious appeal for the young singer. The kids were paid about $1,000 per show and worked like adult actors. But the promise of celebrity fundamentally changed the auditions. Instead of hundreds of kids turning up for a shot at the show, *thousands* of expectant, starry-eyed children mobbed the try-outs.

Alanis, who had already showed a dramatic flair as a supporting cast member in the local production of *Annie*, was part of that stampede. But she says she knew almost nothing about the show when she went to audition. She simply spotted a classified ad calling for kids and, sensing yet another opportunity to perform and develop her skills, she arranged to be there.

"I had never seen the show, but a lot of people there had seen it and they were wondering what I was doing there," Alanis says. Why would someone who didn't know what the show was about bother to audition?

Hagyard recalls that the audition process was frightening and attracted swarms of kids. "It was like being overrun with locusts," she says. "The kids who came on around Alanis's time were aware that they were going to be celebrities. The first kids weren't. They were doing their TV show, and getting paid a whole bunch of money and nobody here ever saw it."

The second wave of kids coming out for auditions seemed more sophisticated, better dressed, and elegantly groomed. At her audition, Alanis was asked to read a few cue cards.

"You're great," the show's talent-finder told her. "But you're too tall."

Alanis grabbed her shoes and left the audition. A staff member called out to her in the hallway.

"You know what? Who cares if you're too tall? Come on back," the staffer said. Alanis was in.

Even among the newly sophisticated hopefuls, Alanis made a different impression. "Alanis didn't fit in, like if one of the Walton kids had gone to finishing school in the city. . . She was young and there was no question she wasn't any older than she looked. But she thought older," Hagyard explains. "She was never a little kid. She was always focused on what she wanted to be. On a show surrounded by kids who are ten through and through, she stood out like a sore thumb. She didn't giggle at stuff."

Even though Hagyard recalls Alanis being more poised and mature, Alanis herself felt it was her lack of TV experience that set her apart. "I was so inexperienced with the whole world of television acting . . . The other cast members were very self-possessed," Alanis says. "I was being integrated into a group of actors that had been together for many years. So that's always tough, especially being integrated into a group that had their dynamic already set up. I was the new kid on the block."

Landing a spot on the show meant being enrolled in acting classes, maintaining a high standard of scholastic achievement, and working long hours after school to create the sketches, which always used the kids' actual names and incorporated some of their natural personality traits into their character. A tough kid offstage became the Bully on the show. A shy kid behind the scenes was Bashful in front of the camera. An awkward kid became Clumsy, fumbling the props.

Alanis naturally became the Mature One. She wasn't part of the core cast (nor part of the promotional excursions), but was a supporting character, the one who was serious about everything — including affairs of the heart.

One early skit had Alanis being confronted by two flower-bearing boys, Matthew and Adam, both evidently interested in asking her out.

"I read in a romance book once that something happened like this and both boys fought each other to see which one would take her out," Alanis teasingly tells the pair.

They agree and begin to wrestle. Adam eventually surrenders. "You win and I lose," he tells a victorious Matthew, who yells good luck and bolts offscreen.

"Adam, I thought you lost!" declares a bewildered Alanis.

"Well, yes. That's the whole idea, Alanis," says a glum Adam. "I lost, so I have to take you out. Where do you want to start?"

Alanis screams in frustration, slams down the flowers, and stomps away.

"Is it something I said, Alanis?" asks Adam, to the sound of canned laughter.

Another recurring sketch had the cast inverting reality, performing everyday tasks backwards and behaving in direct contradiction to normal behaviour. In one of those "opposite sketches," Hagyard, as mother, bawls out Alanis for staying in her room and doing her homework, when she should be out chasing boys.

Although friends say Alanis possessed a sharp wit even then, her devotion to acting left little room for laughs. "I don't even know what kind of sense of humour Alanis has, because she was so dedicated," says Hagyard. "Not solemn, not a not-fun kid, but I never saw her transported."

During the downtime in between shoots, the other kids would bring in games and toys, while Alanis would read or talk about a new record she had picked up. It wasn't that she was aloof. She just didn't have much in common with her co-stars. "Alanis had to learn to do stuff in bad taste," says Hagyard. "If somebody did a really rude thing like burping, she was embarrassed, where everyone else would just laugh because it was breaking the rules."

The show's international distribution brought lots of fan mail. The kids were permitted to read it under supervision, but Alanis's depiction — more mature and slightly above the juvenile fray — was resented by some young viewers. Because the boys on the show pursued Alanis romantically, she received some hate mail, but she made a habit of not reading any letters, good or bad.

To maintain continuity from scene to scene during her time on *You Can't Do That on Television*, Alanis couldn't change her appearance, get her ears pierced, or have her hair radically restyled, for example, without first checking with the show to see if the plot could accommodate the change. That, combined with the fast pace and the long hours, exposed her to what really goes into producing an entertainment spectacle.

In later years, when *You Can't Do That on Television* was resurrected in syndicated repeats, she would laugh at her then tomboyish appearance, but acknowledged the important role the show played in her development. "*You Can't Do That on Television* helped me a lot, because I was working with a lot of other professionals," she told the Carleton Productions documentary crew in 1991. "And just working with them, in the first place, helped me gain experience. The show helped me learn how to be myself in front of a camera and not freeze up. It's good because especially when you are doing videos nowadays, you have to incorporate a lot of your acting skills."

Ultimately, Alanis had a brief run on the show. She figures she appeared on no more than eight episodes. Despite her talent, she was just too mature for a program devoted to childishness, and she wasn't invited back for subsequent seasons.

There would be infrequent acting assignments for Alanis in the future, but the experience on *You Can't Do That on Television* honed her focus. If she was to have a career as an artist, it would be as a singer.

3

Find the
Right Mentor

As Alanis toiled through her TV work, Lindsay Morgan took the $3,000 grant from FACTOR and prepared to make a record.

He turned to his acquaintance Rich Dodson, who had two major qualifications for the job of Alanis's recording engineer and co-producer: the basement of his Toronto-area home housed a twenty-four-track recording studio; and he had proven himself as a hitmaker. Throughout the seventies, Dodson was a member of The Stampeders, one of the first fully made-in-Canada rock success stories, with hits like "Wild Eyes," "Playing in the Band," "New Orleans," and Dodson's classic, "Sweet City Woman." From 1971 to 1974 The Stampeders were the biggest touring Canadian band in the country, with ten top-five hits in Canada and three top-forty hits in the United States.

Morgan hoped that Dodson's accomplishments as a bona fide producer would bring some prestige and sophistication to the project, and so he booked studio time and brought Alanis down to make a record in July 1986, just after her twelfth birthday.

Dodson and Morgan had prepared much of the instrumental track prior to Alanis's arrival. All she needed to do was add her vocals to the two songs selected for the single: "Find the Right Man" and "Fate Stay with Me." Dodson spent two six-hour sessions on separate days recording her vocals.

The circumstances could have been intimidating for a child, working in an unfamiliar setting with complicated recording equipment, under the tutelage of a relative stranger. Alanis seemed tentative at first, but she quickly warmed up and even remembered to flatter her producer by lauding his work with The Stampeders. She wasn't star-struck, though. She was used to working with adults, and besides, with Lindsay ("He was like an uncle to me") and Dodson ("Rich was cool"), Alanis was quickly at ease.

Dodson felt that the songs were impressive, but nothing special. Still, he recognized Alanis possessed talent and ambition well beyond her years and he was impressed by the catalogue of original songs (more than thirty by that point) she had already amassed. "I thought she had very good potential. But I mean, I had a lot of other things on my mind. I wasn't into any long-term commitments. A light didn't go off, saying: 'You must pick up this project.' But I thought she was very good and nice to work with." Above all else, Dodson noticed her determination to succeed: "She wanted to be a big star. No doubt about it. She was very aggressive. Very dedicated."

At the hands of Morgan and Dodson, "Fate Stay with Me" was transformed into a polished pop bauble. Like so many songs of the era, the arrangement leans heavily on synthesizer technology and is a collision of banging drum machines, shimmering layers of keyboards, and chirpy vocals. "Find the Right Man" was given a quasi-reggae beat, but like "Fate Stay with Me," it was aimed squarely at the dance floor, a kind of home-brewed version of Madonna's early hits.

Despite Alanis's talent and dedication, the response from record labels was disheartening. The rejection letters all acknowledged Alanis's qualities, but said the record was destined to fall between the cracks of the record business. Although the songs were aimed at the adult market, their singer was obviously still a child. She couldn't be marketed as a child and she couldn't be marketed as an adult. Among the rejection letters Morgan still has on file is one from MCA Records executive John Alexander, who, within a few years, was to play such an important and long-lasting role in Alanis's career.

Alanis says now that she is sympathetic to the labels' dilemma. "When you are dealing with a twelve-year-old, you are dealing with songs from a children's TV show. And if you are dealing with an adult, you are dealing with someone communicating to their peers. I can understand why they were looking at it and going, what are we going to do with this?"

Even as their plans to attract a record label faltered, Alanis pursued any chance to perform. At Dodson's suggestion, the Morissette family travelled to Toronto so Alanis could audition for the U.S.-based syndicated TV show *Star Search*. She was rejected. She also maintained a steady stream of live performances, singing at the 1986 telethon to benefit the Children's Hospital of Eastern Ontario, and for Ontario's Lieutenant Governor at a May 1986 Girl Guides annual meeting at the Skyline Hotel in Ottawa.

Alanis also made headlines when she performed with Dominic D'Arcy at a year-end assembly at St. Patrick's High School. Dressed in an oversized, shoulder-padded blazer, baggy pants rolled up to mid-calf, and sandals, Alanis struggled with a broken tape recorder before finally launching into "Fate Stay with Me." D'Arcy told the crowd: "A girl with this much talent should not have to leave the city to reach Anne Murray fame. When you get home, I want you to call the radio stations and get them to play 'Fate Stay with Me.' Let's do it here in Ottawa. Let's have a star."

But with no major label interested in helping her become a star, Alanis and Morgan opted to manufacture the record independently, which suited Alanis just fine. Just being able to hold her own record in her hands was as much as she could have dreamed. She didn't care if she sold a single copy. She'd have been happy to give them away.

They started their own record label, Lamor Records. The label's name comprised the letters L and A (for Lindsay and Alanis), and M-O-R (the first three letters of both their names, Morgan and Morissette), and resembled the French word for love (*l'amour*). Through Lamor, Morgan and Alanis worked with Dodson's company, Marigold, and used Morgan's own money and some of the cash Alanis had saved from her work on *You Can't Do That on Television* to print up about 1,300 singles in February 1987. The 45s were shipped out across North America in April 1987, and Morgan hoped the record would land on the desk of someone who would recognize the promise he himself had seen in young Alanis.

Even without major label promotion supporting it, the single did get some favourable response. In his files, Dodson still has surveys conducted by a Kentucky-based company, soliciting opinions from nightclub disc jockeys. One of two surveys rated "Fate Stay with Me" five out of five for "DJ opinion." The record's audience response earned a 4.33 rating out of five. "I love this tune. Sounds like it's crying out to be remixed into a great twelve-inch," one surveyor concluded, referring to the extended mixes favoured by dance clubs. The writer went on to describe "Find the Right Man" as "perfect," and concluded by declaring, "Welcome Alanis."

Despite these encouraging signs, however, it soon became clear that Alanis and Morgan had taken her music as far as they could. "The companies are going to have to market you, and if they feel they can't market you, they can't," he said wistfully.

Morgan had his own career as a country-rock singer to think about, too. When they decided to go their separate ways, Alanis was left without a music business guide, so she and her parents began to search for a new mentor.

▽

Alanis was willing to look for a new mentor anywhere, at any time —
even in church.

When a friend pointed out singer Louise Reny during one Sunday
mass at St. Mary's, Alanis didn't hesitate. Right after the service, she
cornered the singer.

As half of the Ottawa-based synth-pop duo One To One, Reny was
used to young fans pestering her for autographs. But this kid was different. "I want to be a singer," Alanis told Reny. "My parents would like to
talk to you. Can you come over, or can I get your phone number?"

Initially Reny found the request a little odd and hesitated, looking
at the bright young face in front of her. Finally, she reluctantly gave
Alanis her phone number, after getting her to promise not to hand it
out to friends.

Reny and multi-instrumentalist Leslie Howe (the other half of One
To One) had managed to build a modest hit-making reputation out of
Distortion, a studio in the basement of Howe's Ottawa townhouse.
Lifelong friends and at one time husband and wife, Reny and Howe
had entered the music business as part of a cover band, and toured the
country in the early eighties.

In 1985, the pair became One To One and issued *Forward Your
Emotions*, an album reminiscent of Eurythmics and other sleek, tech-
heavy eighties hitmakers. Two songs from it, "There Was a Time" and
the memorable "Angel in My Pocket," became hits, the latter even
garnering the band attention in the United States. By 1987, One To
One was one of the few viable, active recording acts in town. And
if Alanis wanted a role model close to home, witty, attractive, and
talented Louise Reny — whose personality often drew comparisons
to Alanis's other early heroine, Madonna — was a natural. Alanis loved
her voice and was drawn to her charismatic personality.

The Morissettes recognized that their daughter was determined to
succeed as a singer, but that she didn't know what her next move
should be. Should she keep writing songs? Buy more time in the studio? Join a rock band and hit the road? "We felt, if it is a budding talent,
we've got to find the people that can take it further certainly than we

ever could," Alan Morissette told the documentary crew from Carleton Productions in 1991. The opportunities for stardom in Ottawa were limited, and despite her hard work and talent, Alanis's prospects were similarly limited. She needed someone like Reny to advise her about life in the music business.

A week after Alanis tracked Reny down, Georgia Morissette telephoned the singer and spoke with her for half an hour. The conversation ended with Georgia inviting Reny over for brunch.

"So I went. I felt like an idiot. But I just liked Alanis, because she was so sweet," Reny says.

Reny found that although Georgia was promoting her daughter's career, she wasn't prodding Alanis into showbiz. The impetus to perform was Alanis's, and her mother was actively, even aggressively, seeking opportunities to help her realize that goal.

They played "Fate Stay with Me" for Reny and asked where she thought they should go next. Reny herself had been on the road, playing in bands since she was in her mid-teens, and didn't think Alanis, at twelve, should go that route and abandon herself to one-night-stands and low-rent touring.

"I thought, is this what you want to do? I did it when I was fifteen and it kind of wrecked my whole high school life. I had no great memories of the prom. I was always playing. I thought, God, she's only twelve. At least I got to go to junior high and enjoy that."

Keep writing, Reny advised. But forget about joining a band — Alanis was too young.

▽

Georgia found another opportunity for Alanis in the spring of 1987, at a fashionable shop on Sussex Drive, just down the street from the prime minister's residence.

The occasion was a fashion and makeup show at a tony boutique in Ottawa's trendy Byward Market. Georgia had been invited to the show, and while chatting with the other guests, she learned that Stephan

Klovan was there. Klovan was a former figure skating champion and experienced showbiz hand who had recently returned to Ottawa to help produce seasonal festival shows, and he was working on a proposed Bryan Adams homecoming concert. At the show, Adams was to pull a girl from the audience and serenade her. Georgia thought Alanis would be perfect for the part.

After making her way over to Klovan, Georgia broached the subject with him. Alanis could even duet with Adams, she offered. Klovan was polite, but doubted Alanis was suitable for Adams, who was apparently looking for an older girl.

"I said I would check into it. But it wasn't going to happen," Klovan says. But Klovan was also auditioning children for an upcoming kids' show, and he gave Georgia his business card, inviting her to bring her daughter to try out.

Georgia thanked him, and said: "My son is really talented, too — they're twins."

Klovan replied, "Well, bring 'em down."

Dozens of kids turned out for Klovan's audition, but to his surprise, Alanis and Wade Morissette didn't show up. A few days later, Georgia anxiously phoned Klovan, saying she had just discovered his card in her purse, and realized she had missed the audition. She asked if he was holding another, but Klovan wasn't. However, he still needed a few extra kids, and perhaps he could arrange to audition them. The Morissettes were then living close to Klovan, in the Hunt Club community at the southern edge of the city. He agreed to drive over for an after-school audition.

Klovan's background in skating put him in the limelight at a young age, and this probably contributed to the rapport he would develop with Alanis. At ten, he began figure skating competitively and by thirteen, he was competing nationally, later becoming a Junior Canadian Champion. He had opportunities to skate for Canada and, because of his father's roots, for Czechoslovakia. But he was also offered a contract with the organization that had drawn him to the sport as a child: the Ice Capades.

During his five-year run with the Ice Capades, from 1979 to 1984, Klovan says he partnered with Peggy Fleming and Dorothy Hamill, two of the biggest female stars in figure skating. Touring took him around the world, to Las Vegas casinos, work in TV commercials, and even a performance on plastic ice at New York City's notorious Studio 54. But life on the road took its toll, and after some work at coaching and choreography, he decided to return to Ottawa to work on the ice skating specials organized for Winterlude, the city's winter festival. Those shows turned out so well, Klovan was asked to choreograph a kids' show on roller skates for the Festival of Spring, the event he was preparing for when he went over to the Morissette residence for last-minute auditions with Alanis and Wade.

The idea of choreographing kids on roller skates was proving futile. In the days before in-line skates, Klovan found kids could not master the tricky manoeuvres. Even as he arrived at the Morissettes' home, he knew the Festival of Spring show would need to be completely redesigned, and he wanted to see if the Morissette twins would be suitable dancers. When he arrived at the house, Alanis and Wade had just arrived home from school. Alanis dropped her school books on the floor and skipped out to the terrace around the family's pool for the audition.

"She looked just like a nice, fresh girl. She had a nice aura about her. Even from that day, I realized that she was more comfortable around older people," Klovan says.

He showed them a few simple dance steps, and the kids adequately mimicked his moves. Then he asked them each to perform a cartwheel. Alanis levelled her gaze at him and sternly proclaimed: "I don't know if I want to do a cartwheel."

"Listen sweetie, if you want to be in the show, you'll do a cartwheel," Klovan replied.

He showed her how to do a cartwheel, and was impressed with how easily she took his direction and how comfortable she was around a stranger. "Alanis was mature in a lot of ways. We just really connected."

As the audition was winding down, Georgia came out to the yard and announced that Klovan had to hear Alanis sing. He had no plans to include singing in his show, but she was insistent. So Alanis performed a back porch recital of "Find the Right Man." What initially struck Klovan was the unsettling mix of the song's adult message and the singer's childish appearance. He thought the performance was cute, but found the song's subject matter to be a little beyond her years. When he told Alanis what he thought, she countered, "Well, *I* wrote it."

She encored with "Fate Stay with Me," which was much more to Klovan's liking, and gave him a copy of the single.

Klovan listened to the song over and over again at home later that night, and it began to grow on him. "Music has always been an inspiration for me for stylizing a show. In this particular case, with 'Fate Stay with Me,' I thought this is a really cute song, I'm going to use it." In fact, he decided to transform the event into a kids' fashion show-cum-musical revue entirely built around his new discovery, Alanis.

In the following weeks, as Klovan scrambled to redesign the show and run through rehearsals, the Morissettes invited him to watch Alanis compete in a local high school talent show. Unfortunately, Alanis's performance was interrupted when a prop lamp-post fell over and she lost the competition. Klovan seized the moment to pass on some showbiz lessons to Alanis.

"You know, you are really good, but you are really stiff. You have got to loosen up," he told her after the performance — a criticism that visibly stung the young performer. "That's another thing you are going to have to learn if you are going to work with somebody like me. You have to take constructive criticism," he warned.

They set to work on the festival show, with both Alanis and Wade as featured performers. But the main ingredient would be Alanis's "Fate Stay with Me." To help her relax, Klovan put her in front of a mirror and videotaped her performance so she could study her mistakes. "I basically worked with her like a skater without skates."

At last, he had rehearsed his crew of kids into polished performers. Even if his show didn't have the resources of a Las Vegas revue, Klovan managed to get the kids to strive for a professional standard of excellence. Decked out in a bright yellow dress and surrounded by a cast of supporting dancers, Alanis belted out a tune like a seasoned veteran. Audiences, mostly made up of school kids bussed in for the shows, were captivated.

"I ended up making her the star of that little production," says Klovan. "I knew that she had a lot of potential. It was just a gut feeling I had. And I was right."

Alanis was in her element, loving the opportunity to be onstage, performing in front of an audience. "At that time, I was performing for the sake of the high that one gets from being up onstage," she says.

Krysia Kehoe, who was dating Alanis's older brother Chad, was invited along to the performance and was impressed by her boyfriend's kid sister: "I was floored. I said: 'This little body is really bellowing.' A good voice, really going strong."

Working so closely with the teen gave Klovan the opportunity to see that Alanis was more than just precocious. She was mature well beyond her years and she had what he calls that "special spark." After rehearsals, he would take her to Dairy Queen for an ice cream, and they would talk about everything, including her desire for a career as an entertainer. "We just connected a lot. We spoke the same language. She was really eager to learn and I was able to give her a lot of information." Klovan had auditioned a lot of kids for that show, and a lot of performers over the years, and he knew Alanis "had it." He sensed something right off the bat. "There's sort of a sixth sense you have in the entertainment business. She definitely had an undefinable quality. I guess you could say star quality."

After the Festival of Spring show, Alanis's parents talked with Klovan about becoming her manager. They had been trying to advance her career, but knew that they needed someone in the business to take over. Klovan liked the idea, but felt that the family was only interested in his services if the other Morissette kids could have careers in show business as well. "We went through a period where Alanis's dad was really insistent, that if I was going to do it, I had to treat all three kids the same," Klovan recalls.

Other sources say it's true that Alanis and Wade yearned to be onstage, but don't recall Chad, Alan, or Georgia ever expressing any desire to enlist all three kids in the arts. But Klovan says Chad eventually conceded he wasn't really interested, and he asked Wade to seriously consider whether he was ready to make the commitment to life as an entertainer. And after consulting an entertainment lawyer in Toronto, he waited for the situation to sort itself out.

"It was my first time. I was not sure what I was doing, to be honest," he says of his new role. Alanis was eager to lighten the burden her career was placing on her parents, and the easiest way to do that was to work with someone like Klovan: "The best thing to do at the time was to work with somebody from outside my family who was inspired, who was passionate about what I knew about music at the time."

Klovan says he signed a formal management contract, although Alanis says there was no contract. At any rate, he ultimately assumed the role of manager and agent for Alanis, grooming her for a career in show business. His decision to work with Alanis was not based purely on her talent, however. The stable and nurturing environment of the Morissette household was the deciding factor. In his skating days, Klovan had watched promising careers come undone under financial or personal strain, and if he was going to leap into the hurly-burly world of showbiz with a teenager, he wanted to make sure she had plenty of support.

"One thing I liked about getting involved with Alanis's family is they are very solid. It wasn't a dysfunctional family. Financially sound. All the ingredients were there for me to get involved with her."

Klovan says his professional relationship with Alanis naturally evolved into a close relationship with her family, and he often stayed for dinner after rehearsals at the Morissette home. As a dinner guest, he witnessed the family's peculiar ritual of taking turns sharing their thoughts and feelings at the end of each day. "If you weren't used to it, you might think it was kind of weird," he concedes. But he admired the Morissettes for their openness and enjoyed being in their warm and loving family environment.

This environment provided a good base for Alanis. Although she

ALANIS

FATE STAY WITH ME

▲ The cover of Alanis's first single, "Fate Stay with Me," "Find the Right Man." *Courtesy Lindsay Morgan*

▼ Outtakes from Alanis's photo session for the "Fate Stay with Me" single cover. *Courtesy Lindsay Morgan*

▲
Dominic D'Arcy (with guitar), Ottawa's Singing Policeman, leads Alanis and Wade Morissette in song at a performance at the Children's Hospital of Eastern Ontario in Ottawa, in the mid-1980s.
Courtesy Dominic D'Arcy

Alanis prepared this ▶ handwritten list of songs she performed at charity events in Ottawa in the mid-to-late 1980s. The top half, marked "mine," are songs Alanis wrote herself. The bottom half are popular cover tunes she liked to sing. *Courtesy Stephan Klovan*

Song list (Alanis)

mine {
Fate Stay With Me
Find the Right Man
I Gotta Go
Another Sleepless Night
Your Dream Has Come On Tim
Over Now (?)
Get With It
Toughen Up
This Feeling
Be There as My Friend

The Rose
Summertime
I Can't Help Falling In Love
Hotel California
Flashdance
Strut
Summertime Blues

▲ Alanis and her twin
brother Wade pose for
Dalmy's Kids in the
1988 Dalmy's catalogue.
The twins became known
as the Dalmy's Kids and
performed at store
openings in Canada.
*Reitmans Inc. (Smart Set –
Dalmy's Division)*

◀ Backstage with local
news anchor Max
Keeping at a fashion
show in September
1991. Ottawa Sun

Alanis models
clothes and sings
at a fashion show at
the Westin Hotel,
Ottawa. *Stephan Klovan*

▲ The cover of Alanis's first Canadian album, *Alanis* (1991). *MCA Music Publishing*

◀ Alanis laughs as she tries on clothes during a trip to New York. *Stephan Klovan*

Likely taken during her early concert performance opening an Ottawa show for Vanilla Ice at Frank Clair Stadium. *Anita Antonucci*, Ottawa Sun

▶

Alanis performs the national anthem at an Ottawa Rough Riders football game at Frank Clair Stadium on August 8, 1991. *Peter Cutler*, Ottawa Sun

Alanis and
her mother, Georgia,
relax during the game at
▲ Frank Clair Stadium. *Stephan Klovan*

At the climax of her August 1991 half-time show,
Alanis is hoisted on high by two male dancers, as
cheerleaders in the foreground strike a pose.
Moments after this photo was taken,
Alanis was presented with her
first gold record. *Mark
Webster*, Ottawa Sun
▼

Aerobics with The King? Alanis stretches out in November 1991 at "Attitude Flex,"
a benefit to promote fitness activities for adults with disabilities, at the
Canadian Museum of Nature. Alanis's T-shirt reads "Attitude Is Everything."
Moe Doiron, Ottawa Sun

was ready to step into the spotlight, even then, she understood the hazards of jealousy from her siblings and peers. And so she downplayed whatever she was doing, trying to maintain a balance between remaining humble and allowing herself the luxury of appreciating her own accomplishments.

"There is a fine line between humility and depriving yourself of celebrating how far you have come creatively. I walk that line all the time," she says now. Whatever her early strategy for normalizing school and home relations, it evidently worked. "I never, ever sensed any jealousy from the brothers at all," says Klovan. "They were all strong in their way."

Although his main job was to find outlets for Alanis, Klovan quickly landed both Alanis and Wade opportunities. The regional manager for the Dalmy's Kids clothing store chain had seen the Festival of Spring show and asked Klovan to design shows for the clothing franchise. He immediately seized on the chance to showcase his new discovery. "I presented the idea of Alanis and Wade as the Dalmy's Kids. That was a big break."

Soon she and her brother were featured in shopping mall posters and ads for the retail outfit. Klovan also convinced the chain's marketing director to let Alanis have a shot at composing Dalmy's theme song.

The marketing director came to Ottawa to meet with Klovan and Alanis and tossed around ideas for the song. Alanis went off, came up with lyrics and a melody, and Klovan took it to the company, which agreed to finance a recording session.

"It wasn't very fair/Seemed mothers did not care/There was a store for them, not me/But now the time has come/Us kids are number one," went the lyrics. The song was used as a radio jingle, and whenever a new Dalmy's store would open, Alanis and Wade, with Klovan as chaperone, were flown in to dance and sing for customers. The job didn't pay much, but all their expenses were covered, and the kids considered the trips a holiday.

At each stop, Alanis would sing a few songs, and with Wade, she'd perform a routine choreographed by Klovan. "That started giving her experience. She started getting opportunities and really liked it," says Klovan.

Alanis's career got a further boost in the summer of 1987, when she entered Youth Talent Search '87, a locally televised talent contest. Dressed in an acid-wash denim jacket and skirt, she chirped through "Fate Stay with Me" and was named grand prize winner. "I want to prove to people that just because you're young, it doesn't mean you can't do as much as adults can," she told *Ottawa Magazine* in a profile later that summer.

Soon, Klovan was spending almost every day of the week at the Morissette home. He and Alanis would spend hours practising dance routines, experimenting with different fashion looks, and debating what kind of image they wanted to present. "At that time, Debbie Gibson and Tiffany were really big items in the States," Klovan says, referring to two adolescents who enjoyed a brief run up and down the charts. "Alanis was in that age group, so we were targeting the same market in Canada."

Klovan admits he knew little about the music business at the time. He assumed that if Alanis wanted to be a musician, she needed formal voice and music composition lessons. Then he learned that in contemporary music, the inability to read music and lack of formal voice training were no impediment to success. After a few sessions, they decided the lessons were unnecessary.

But there was one thing Klovan *could* teach Alanis. From his experience in ice shows, he had developed a particular kind of attitude about being a professional artist and entertainer. He had observed how temperamental skaters let their private lives affect their work on ice or on camera, but Klovan earned a reputation as someone who left his problems behind when performing. "I was a very versatile type of performer. I was never sick. I was very reliable," Klovan says of his skating days. Performing well, putting on a proper show, earning a reputation as a reliable professional were all about maintaining a veneer of glamour, effortless charm, and, above all else, a big, happy smile. Like competitive figure skaters who sport an ear-to-ear grin despite any pain, Alanis would become a hard-working, happy-looking crowd pleaser under Klovan's tutelage. From this point forward, she would equate performing with repressing whatever stress and anxiety she might be experiencing. Whatever adolescent torment she would encounter in the coming years would have to wait. When she was onstage, Alanis would greet the world with a smile. No matter what. "I was prepared to entertain people and perform, as opposed to being naked and unadulterated and honest," she says.

Klovan may have had the talent and connections to make Alanis a star, but she still needed help becoming a musician. She and Klovan were on the lookout for someone to work with on her music — and it wasn't long before fate would prove to stay with Alanis once again.

Her mother happened to overhear someone at a restaurant mention the name of Leslie Howe, Louise Reny's instrumental partner in One To One. Georgia asked if the man knew Howe, and it turned out he did. They exchanged phone numbers and arranged for Howe to receive a tape of Alanis's songs.

Howe, who at the time was unaware of Reny's previous meeting with the Morissettes, liked the tape, which included Alanis's performance of Bette Midler's song "The Rose." He invited the Morissettes over to his studio for further discussion. Howe thought she had a fine voice for someone so young, but knew any shot at success would not come overnight. This was a talent that would need to be developed over time. But he liked her attitude and found her to be uncharacteristically "cool" for a thirteen-year-old. "I knew it would take a lot of work and practice and stuff like that. But I thought it could develop into something."

As Klovan saw it, Howe's track record with One To One made him "pretty hip and happening," but more importantly, he was the only likely candidate in town. "Really, at the time, there was no real money to do anything on a bigger scale. We were all kind of feeling things out," says Klovan. A promotional flyer for Howe's forty-eight-track studio, Distortion, declared it a "world-class recording facility" with a "vast selection of MIDI instruments, samplers, sequencers and sounds." Rental fees were $60 per hour, plus $20 for an engineer.

Alanis immediately felt comfortable in Howe's working environment, and she admired Reny, who was still collaborating with Howe in One To One. "(Howe) was pretty damn open and curious," recalls Alanis. "It was just great to be in a studio again. And to potentially write songs was such an exciting notion, it sounded like a great idea."

Howe wasn't on the lookout for a young singer to mould for stardom. He was still mostly focused on his own career. Nevertheless, he decided to begin a parallel career collaborating with Alanis. "This girl is good, she can sing, she has talent, she's got a great personality, and great looks. Perhaps we can do something together," he said.

On October 8, 1988, Howe drew up a personal services contract with his company, Ghettovale Productions. Alanis signed, and because she was a minor, so did her dad. The contract made Howe Alanis's producer for up to five albums.

Signing such contracts can be scary for new recording artists. They entail nothing less than blind faith and complete trust, and, consequently, can be a source of regret for some artists an album or two down the road. But for Alanis, the contract represented an opportunity she was anxious and excited to take. "Here was someone that was conceivably going to spend a lot of time and perhaps a lot of his own money and . . . it would only make sense he would want a contract signed," says Alanis. "I wanted to write music. I wanted to get a record together. I wanted to get songs together for an album."

Their goal now was to write songs, license a record to a major label, and make Alanis a star.

4

Friends in
High Places

With Howe and Alanis now committed to creating music in the privacy of the studio, Klovan began to seek out more opportunities for her to perform in public. Since Ottawa is the ultimate political town, Klovan decided to put that to work for Alanis. Soon he hit on a unique venue that would gain the young singer exposure: performing the national anthem at high-profile events. And in a city like Ottawa, there's no shortage of gatherings that require the patriotic charge of a well-performed rendition of "O Canada."

Her first opportunity came with the 1988 World Cup of Figure Skating, which was being held in Ottawa that October. Klovan was working on a TV special with Ottawa-based Olympic figure skating medalist Elizabeth Manley when producers of the championship asked

him to arrange for a recording of "O Canada" for the opening ceremonies. The producers weren't even thinking about having the anthem
performed, they just wanted Klovan to track down a recording.

"I can do better than that," Klovan said. "I've got this thirteen-year-
old girl who can sing her heart out. How about giving her a shot at it?"

The producer agreed but told Klovan that it better be good: "It's
really, really important."

Klovan realized this was a great opportunity to make an impression,
but Alanis couldn't sing the anthem any old way. He enlisted Howe to
come up with a new backing track to accompany Alanis at the ceremony. Howe in turn asked his friend Frank Levin, keyboardist with the
Ottawa band Eight Seconds, to come up with the instrumental, which
Klovan described as "a pumped-up version of 'O Canada,'" with a little
bit of a "rock flavour" to it. Giving the anthem an untraditional rock
twist could have failed miserably, but Klovan was hopeful that Alanis,
with his coaching, would rise to the occasion.

In preparing Alanis for the performance, Klovan followed the same
strategy he had used with young skaters. Just before she was called
out to stand in the spotlight at centre ice, he psyched her up with
encouragement, right up until the moment she stepped out into the
arena. And the technique worked. Alanis's performance was so moving, a uniformed RCMP officer on hand for the ceremony wept. Klovan
was later besieged by skaters and judges congratulating him on his
new discovery. "I knew right then that that was a good vehicle for her."

Another of Klovan's strategies was to introduce young Alanis to the
influential members of Ottawa society. And the easiest way to do that
was to make her performance of "O Canada" part of the proceedings
whenever Klovan was called upon to organize a party. *Ottawa Citizen*
reporter Margo Roston wrote about one of these events in a March 9,
1989, society column. The occasion was a special screening of the
Elizabeth Manley CBC TV special, *Dear Elizabeth*, and the party was
organized by none other than Klovan at the Westin Hotel. Roston
reported the shindig had "Ottawa-style razzle dazzle, with RCMP
outriders at the ballroom door, a champagne reception, a screen

surrounded by a lighted rainbow, a jazzy rendition of 'O Canada' sung by 14-year-old Alanis, a fur fashion show and an array of inviting desserts." Another event Klovan organized, a benefit for the Ronald McDonald House charity, was written up in the *Citizen* a few months later: "The show will feature Natalie Tessier, world baton twirler champion for girls six and under, and Alana (sic) Morissette."

Ranking a mention above the desserts but below the lighted rainbow or having your misspelled name listed lower on the marquee than a baton twirler was not exactly taking the town by storm. But soon, Alanis would become synonymous with "O Canada" in Ottawa, appearing everywhere from political dinners to pro football games. She was now the Anthem Girl.

It was a repetitive routine, getting dressed up, meeting a new group of adult strangers, awaiting introduction, singing the same song, and then waiting until enough time had passed to leave politely. But Klovan says performing for up to tens of thousands of spectators can only have boosted Alanis's confidence. "It certainly hasn't hurt her. I think she realizes that now." And Alanis told the documentary film crew from Carleton Productions in 1991 that she genuinely enjoyed singing "O Canada," believing it was an extension of her sincere patriotism. "It's not just, oh, I'm singing the national anthem. It's like I'm singing for Canada. It's important to me, and I love this country. When I say I love Canada and that I want to stay in Ottawa, I'm not just saying that to sound patriotic. I mean it."

Apart from "O Canada," Alanis's repertoire of cover songs was expanding, and she began singing at fashion shows and charity events around the city. Klovan still has tapes of canned backing tracks she would sing along to at some events: Madonna's "Cherish" and "Crazy for You," Donna Summer's "She Works Hard for Her Money," Ben E. King's "Stand By Me," Janet Jackson's "What Have You Done for Me Lately," the Eagles' "Take It to the Limit" and "Hotel California," the Bangles' "Walk Like an Egyptian," Tina Turner's "What You Get Is What You See," and Olivia Newton-John's *Grease* hit, "Hopelessly Devoted to You."

Meanwhile, her anthem performances were taking her a little farther afield. In the summer of 1989, Klovan brought Alanis to Quebec City, where she opened for pianist André Gagnon. Later, she sang the national anthem on board a military ship loaded with sailors, and judging by their leering reaction, Klovan recognized his client was becoming a beautiful young woman.

"The guys had been out to sea too long," says Klovan. "She looked beautiful. I remember coming on deck with her and it was like Gina Lollobrigida had just walked on board." Yet Alanis was completely comfortable drawing stares. After all, the whole point was to be the centre of attention.

But even if her looks gave off the aura of maturity, she was still a kid at heart and still enjoyed childish pranks. When she got back to the hotel after performing for the sailors, she stole Klovan's shaving cream, slipped into his room, and emptied the can into his bed — the first of many pranks they would play on each other. In fact, the two had so much fun together that people used to wonder about what kind of relationship Alanis and Klovan had. They always seemed to be laughing, like they had a secret joke on everybody. Perhaps they got along so well because Klovan didn't talk down to Alanis; he didn't treat her like a child. And having started performing at a young age himself, he knew the pressures she was facing.

When stuck in hotels in strange cities, she and Klovan would pass the time by turning down the TV volume and making up their own dialogue for bad, late night movies. Klovan also liked to take the underaged teen out nightclubbing when they were on the road, simply to dance and give her a taste of adult fun. Alanis's blossoming good looks and sophisticated wardrobe (courtesy of the modelling work Klovan got her) enabled her to get into the clubs but would often attract the attention of older men, so the pair worked up an elaborate scheme to deflect that attention. They adopted as aliases the names of the villains from the old Rocky and Bullwinkle cartoons, and when someone hit on either one of them, he became Boris and she was Natasha. Their outlandish, invented personal histories would confuse their suitors, who would usually back off. They also took to calling each other Pukoo, although Klovan can't recall why. "We just called each other Pukoo Sr. and Jr. I don't know where it came from."

The work as anthem singer and entertainer wasn't great, but Alanis says the gigs gave her a foot in the door at all kinds of events and let her meet all kinds of people. Soon Klovan began receiving requests to book Alanis for any major political or sporting event, which, curiously, endeared her to the family of then prime minister Brian Mulroney. The Ottawa-Carleton Economic Development Corporation frequently hosted lunches and dinners with dignitaries from across Canada, and Mulroney was often invited to speak. After performing at such functions, Alanis would be invited to sit at the head table with the prime minister and other dignitaries. There she met Mulroney's wife, Mila, who invited the singer to their home — the prime minister's official residence at 24 Sussex Drive — to spend some time with their teenage daughter, Caroline.

Klovan says a few weeks after the invitation, he and Alanis were summoned, and he waited in the library while Alanis hung out with Mulroney's daughter. But Alanis claims to have only vague memories of this occasion now.

▽

While Alanis was maintaining a busy schedule of public appearances, Howe commissioned Louise Reny and Frank Levin to write some new material for her to record. Howe also suggested that Alanis cut some demos of old One To One material, including Reny's "Angel in My Pocket," to acclimatize her to the studio environment. And very soon, Klovan would need that new material. Alanis was to audition once again for *Star Search*, with the hope of landing a spot on international television and winning a $50,000 prize.

Klovan had called the show and boasted about a "really hot young person" he had for the contest's teen category, and they were invited to the show's upcoming auditions in nearby Montreal. The *Star Search* audition was a nerve-wracking experience. Contestants had to follow detailed instructions about what songs they could cover (a ballad and an up-tempo number), the length of the track, the length of the intro — enough stipulations to fill pages. Howe and Levin prepared a remake of The Osmonds' old hit, "One Bad Apple," with a techno-dance arrangement Levin describes as "all funky and Paula Abdul-y."

With the tape in hand, Klovan and Alanis travelled to Montreal for the audition. Normally, contestants entered a professionally lit room and performed before a video camera and a *Star Search* scout, without the presence of a parent or coach. But Klovan managed to talk his way into the session, and they worked out a series of hand gestures so he could silently coach Alanis through the songs.

She performed excellent versions of "One Bad Apple" and a Whitney Houston ballad and Klovan was confident she had landed a spot on the show. But they were shocked by the casting director's reaction. She informed them that the Whitney Houston song was "not allowed" and said they were "going to blow it."

With Alanis looking on, Klovan insisted that there must have been some mistake. The Whitney Houston song was on the list he received. "Too bad," the woman replied. "You came all this way for nothing."

Klovan asked Alanis to step out into the hallway, and then he blew his stack at the director, reproaching her for not having the tact or courtesy to consider the young singer's feelings. "If you are going to do this job, you better learn to deal with it, and I really don't appreciate the way you talked to Alanis!"

The woman apologized and assured Klovan she would send the package off to Los Angeles for consideration.

After the audition, Klovan cheered Alanis up with another nightlife adventure in Montreal, taking her to the cavernous disco Metropolis. The two of them stayed out until early morning, dancing away all the stress of the day.

Back in Ottawa, Alanis, Levin, and Howe cut a newer version of "One Bad Apple," and Klovan decided it wouldn't hurt her chances of being accepted on *Star Search* if she personally delivered the finished tape to the show's offices in New York. He had to travel to the city for some promotional work with the Ice Capades anyway, and was able to sell Alan and Georgia Morissette on the idea of bringing her along. "It is always good to meet Alanis. When people meet her, they really take to her."

While squiring her around the Big Apple, Klovan decided they should do some shopping, and he saw an early indication of Alanis's emerging fashion sense, a tendency towards dressing down that would return much later with *Jagged Little Pill*. He steered her towards high-end fashions at Saks Fifth Avenue, but she was much more interested in exploring the retro looks found in Greenwich Village. When Klovan suggested she try on a hat, Alanis informed him: "I'm not a hat chick." As Klovan says, "She had a definite idea of what she wanted to be seen in and how she wanted to look and what she was comfortable in."

The pair stopped by the New York *Star Search* offices and schmoozed with a casting director, who accepted the tape and promised to send it off to Los Angeles with the rest of the material being considered for the show. Upon leaving, Klovan shrewdly left his sunglasses behind. When he crept back in to retrieve them, the *Star Search* staffer had already cranked Alanis's "One Bad Apple," and was dancing around her office. But Klovan didn't stop there; he followed up with a letter to *Star Search's* talent coordinator, offering to meet with her and to provide even more Alanis material, as well as suggesting they set up a "formal" audition for her. By the spring, Alanis received word that she had won a spot on the second show of the season, to be filmed in Los Angeles.

Winning a spot on *Star Search* was potentially lucrative, but competing was costly. Singing contestants had to prepare enough material to cover them in the event that they won week after week and made it to the finals. That meant Alanis had to prepare twelve songs — a whole album's worth. Her own demos and musical charts of the songs had to be prepared ahead of time and sent to the show's musical director, who then rearranged the song for the show's own band. And all the material had to be drawn from *Star Search's* restrictive catalogue of songs. In return, Alanis was only guaranteed a $900 performing fee and an all-expenses-paid trip to California.

When it came time to perform, Alanis belted out "One Bad Apple," competing against the returning champion, a young cowboy singer named Chad. But despite her high hopes and effort, she lost. Klovan says Team Alanis's strategy had been to save her best material for later in the show, assuming she would win the first round, and that proved to be the wrong way to play it. "One Bad Apple" was not her strongest number, and it ended up being the only one she'd get to sing on *Star Search*.

Alanis handled the defeat well and Klovan was also there to provide support. He knew that even if it ended in defeat, it would be a good experience for her. "Don't even think about winning or losing," he told her beforehand. "You're on an internationally syndicated show." Gaining exposure was the real goal and the two were succeeding at it.

Alanis now dates her own ambivalence about artistic awards (including her contemporary triumphs) to the *Star Search* experience. "They are making children believe that one of these people is better than the other . . . The whole concept of competition within music is such a weird concept to me. At the time it was, too . . . I can't see why they would have to be compared."

▽

With Klovan seeking out opportunities for Alanis and Howe spending long hours working up songs with her in the studio, it's difficult to determine the division of labour between the two men. Klovan called himself her manager, but took the role usually fulfilled by an agent, tracking down performing opportunities. Howe called himself producer, but his influence extended to every aspect of her career: co-writing songs, producing her records, coaching her musical development, and searching for a major label record deal.

The two appeared to be on a collision course, but Klovan says the friction was positive. Howe played the devil's advocate, skeptical and cautious about involving Alanis in anything risky or ill-conceived. Klovan had a more cavalier attitude, ready to take risks and accept any promising opportunity that came their way. "We were good for Alanis," Klovan says. "If Leslie saw a cup, he would say it was half empty, where I would say it was half full."

Initially the two disagreed over whether Alanis should be strictly a studio act like One To One, or whether she should develop as a live performer. "I always wondered how you could be successful if you don't get out and sell your product," Klovan comments. "You don't just train as a skater and not perform physically. It seemed to me, here was this great recording group (One To One) but they never made any appearances." Similarly, Alanis was recording in the studio, but never performed her material anywhere. Klovan felt that discouraging Alanis from performing live would mean that opportunities would slip away from them. But he says he respected Howe's experience and opinion about what direction they should take.

From Howe's perspective, the whole reason for getting involved with Alanis was to make her a recording star, and that meant sticking to studio work: "The whole focus was to try to get a record deal." Although Howe seemed to think singing the national anthem and cover tunes was okay, all the live performance stuff was "secondary."

Klovan even had doubts about Howe's company name, Ghettovale, and thought Alanis should only be associated with an outfit that conveyed success. When asked about Klovan's involvement, Howe is dismissive: "Stephan Klovan more or less had nothing to do with her once I started working with her. Call him an agent. In terms of getting her shows and acting as an agent. In terms of her development, he had nothing, basically, to do with her. I know he likes to take a lot of credit for it."

Klovan remarks that if he ever had another client he would try to "harness control over everything." He now believes "a producer shouldn't necessarily oversee what the management wants to do, he should work for it. But because I was a novice manager, I was tending to lean more with his opinion at the time."

The disputes meant the young singer was often stuck in the middle, even when it came to deciding on her musical approach, her sound. The disagreements never really escalated into arguments, but Alanis would often be torn by the two competing interests. "She had a vision, but she didn't really know what to do with it. She needed help and guidance and that's all I was trying to do," Klovan asserts. Howe says there was no need for aimless discussions about Alanis's career. She was a fourteen-year-old girl, so she would make the kinds of records fourteen-year-old girls enjoyed. "What other type of music would we do?"

And as Reny points out, the fact that Howe didn't even like dance music shows that he wasn't forcing Alanis to do anything she didn't want to. One To One was influenced more by eighties pop acts like the Thompson Twins. Alanis was leaning towards a Janet Jackson–like sound.

Klovan's preference for polished performers and Howe's commercial sensibility, combined with Alanis's willingness to accept the advice of her more experienced collaborators, evolved into a particular kind of image for the young singer: "Someone impenetrable and charismatic and charming and poised and pretty," according to Alanis. "At the time, that was my only perspective as well. And I was looking up to a lot of adults who were honing my skills, even though sometimes it's questionable whether they were doing that or not." She says she didn't always agree that the adults around her advised her to do what was really best. She sometimes felt that their advice meant "a little too much giving in to what society expected." But Alanis now concedes that "at the time I was not old enough or confident enough to express that."

The strategy of having Alanis make highly commercial, slickly packaged music would soon provide an express ride to the top of the charts in Canada. What was missing, though, was the chance for Alanis to develop her own personal artistic voice. The frustrations and turmoil the coming years would bring could have found a perfect outlet in her music. But the music she would make and the performances she would give would be a denial of those emotions.

Over the years, her failure to confront her problems would gnaw away at her until those feelings overwhelmed her life and demanded attention. But for now, Alanis's attention was focused on listening to her collaborators and making it to the top.

5

Paris in the Spring

O n the late night streets of Paris, a crowd was gathering near a fountain at the École Militaire, straining to see what exactly was going on. A pretty young girl dressed only in a bathing suit was frolicking in the fountain and lip-synching to some dance music. On the dry perimeter of the fountain, behind the lights and cameras, stood three men smiling and watching the action. Alanis was making her first video, "I'll Walk Away."

The Alanis braintrust had decided that the swiftest route to a record deal was to finance a video independently and shoot it in a far-flung setting. It was a highly unusual, audacious move. Normally, artists submit to record labels demo audiotapes of their material that they themselves have financed and recorded, which is usually expensive enough. The cost of making a flashy video, especially one shot in a foreign location, is well beyond the grasp of most independent artists. But because so much of Alanis's music was created with keyboards and computer-sequenced, programmed rhythms, Leslie Howe and Stephan Klovan agreed a video was the best way to showcase her, rather than attempting to recreate the sound live, in a club setting. Also, record labels at the time were looking for a more sophisticated promotional package, and they hoped the video would make the right impression.

Once the team settled on the notion of a video, they needed a location. They considered returning to scenic Quebec City, and even talked about travelling to Budapest (apparently because of Georgia Morissette's roots in Hungary), but felt they needed a spot with easily recognizable landmarks. They settled on Paris because it had plenty of readily identifiable sites, and because placing Alanis in that environment would give her the mystique of success and worldliness, says Klovan. Filming Alanis dancing around the Eiffel Tower would make it look like she already had it made: "We felt we had to give Alanis an international, street-smart look, as if she was this hot rock chick who had been around the block a few times. We didn't want to play up the part that she came from this perfect Catholic family."

Before they could do the video at all, however, they had to arrange for some financing, and so an "investment portfolio" was prepared to attract funding for the Paris video shoot. A letter dated April 4, 1989, addressed "Dear potential investor" and signed by Howe, states: "We feel extremely confident at the prospects of securing an international recording and publishing contract; however, at the present, we lack the necessary funds to properly assemble a promotional package to present to these companies.

"We believe it is absolutely imperative to include a promotional video of Alanis in our presentation, to be filmed in Paris . . . This amount, plus generous interest, would be repayable upon the signing of the aforementioned contracts."

The investment package included a budget for the video: $15,110, including $2,610 to fly the three of them, plus a director, to Paris,

$1,740 for accommodation, $1,250 for food, $550 for a Paris stylist, $1,075 for wardrobe, and $325 for dance lessons.

And an attached biography shows the lengths to which they would go to conjure a new identity for Alanis. It had her born in 1975 (a year late) and asserted: "Okay, so she's 14. It's not her fault. She expects to be taken seriously on her own merits. No, she's not a manufactured studio prop, but a multi-talented artist in her own right . . . She has been involved in dance since an early age, giving her a deceivingly mature look in live performance . . . Despite her Grade 9 status, Alanis is a mature young girl with strong ambitions and beaming confidence . . . One is easily fascinated at the thought of her age."

While the document initially played up her youth, under the heading "marketing," it seemed unable to decide whether Alanis's age was a selling point or a liability: "We want to downplay her age and have her be perceived as she is; a multi-talented artist. Yes, we do want people to know her age, but this should not be the focus of her image . . . Alanis's family background is from Hungary, where she lived when she was younger."

This last sentence is fiction. While it is true Georgia was born in Hungary and Alanis made a brief, early childhood visit there, she never lived in her mother's homeland. The document continues, "We plan to exploit these European roots. We want her to be perceived as coming from a lower-middle class European environment . . . Alanis's image will be that of a spunky, street-cool European young woman; singing with meaning and an aggressive, mature attitude. Clothing would be East meets West, with possibly some elements of traditional Hungarian styling along with a street-wise European look. We wish to give the impression of integrity, sincerity and not too happy or bubbly."

Alanis didn't know about the document and now laughs at the contents ("that is so intense!"), but isn't surprised that there was an attempt to conjure up a mysterious persona for her. "Leslie and a couple of other people thought who I was at the time wasn't going to be grandiose enough. And I remember being really opposed to that notion. It never came to fruition," she says. "A lot of people think it has to be greater than the truth in order for it to be charismatic and sought-after. The truth is, if you are what you are and your path is such that you will connect with a lot of people, you will. And if you don't, you were not supposed to."

Klovan says they ultimately made the overseas shoot possible by accepting sponsorship from organizations like Hilton International in Paris (which provided hotel rooms in return for exposure in the clip), along with about $1,000 Alanis won in a contest sponsored by Ottawa radio station Energy 1200, and small donations from local people eager to help out. But the biggest investor, with the most to lose, was Leslie Howe. He was already on the hook with big loans to pay for his recording studio equipment, but says he had enough faith in Alanis's talent to risk running up a huge debt. Counting credit card bills and loans from his father, he estimates he owed about $100,000, and believes if the Alanis project never paid off, he could have lost his studio. For Howe, a lot was riding on whether the Paris video would result in a record deal. "Looking back, it was a little too gutsy . . . Considering my resources, I went a little overboard."

Alanis, Howe, and the director, Denis Beauchamp, arrived in Paris a little bit ahead of Klovan. By the time he met up with them, he found the shoot had not gotten off to a flying start. There were disagreements over how things were supposed to look and how things were supposed to be managed. Alanis was relieved when Klovan arrived, and he quickly realized someone had to step in and take control. So he cast himself as "ringleader and organizer" and began to plan the next day's shoot. "There were too many chiefs and not enough Indians. It wasn't a matter of who is right and who is wrong. It's just that we weren't going to waste five days in Paris being disorganized."

Alanis, who looked up to Klovan as a "big brother," asked to stay in his room on his first night there. The group had agreed to get a full night's sleep, because they had an early shoot the next day, but Klovan decided Alanis needed some relief from the stress. After everyone had retired to their rooms, Klovan looked at Alanis and announced, "We're going out tonight." Boris and Natasha were back in business.

Klovan had previously trained in Paris and knew people in the city. He called a friend who worked at the discothèque Le Palais and got their names on the guest list. They arrived to find a huge lineup, but because of Klovan's connections, they brushed right past all the people. Inside was a lavish, jet-set scene ("It was $25 for a glass of water," Klovan laughs), but the pair got a seat in the corner and joined in the spectacle. They went out club-hopping until 3 a.m. and then made it back to their hotel for a 7 a.m. breakfast meeting.

When they arrived at the table, Howe looked at them and said, "We're so glad you got a good night's sleep. You look so fresh." And the stylist who later came to do Alanis's makeup commented, "Oh, you got a good night's rest." Klovan and Alanis had a private laugh. They had only had about two hours' sleep.

"But we were rested because we had burned off a lot of energy," Klovan remembers. "It was really funny. They had all been to bed and looked like shit!"

The shoot began, with Klovan, Howe, and Beauchamp ("The Three Stooges," says Klovan) framing Alanis against Parisian scenery. But the disagreements continued. Klovan says Howe favoured setting up in dark, moody alleys, while he argued that they could have stayed in Ottawa to film in alleys. "We came all the way to Paris, and we're not shooting Paris. What are we doing here?" Klovan asked in exasperation.

He steered the production towards Notre Dame, Montmartre, and other distinctive locales, but they also kept the concept loose enough to accommodate any improvised ideas. "I'll Walk Away" had been written by Reny with Howe and Levin (Alanis is credited on the final CD version), but there was no narrative structure to the video. Klovan says the idea was to give the clip a spontaneous and fun look. "We were going with the moment. If we were on our way somewhere, and we saw something we really liked, we might go there instead."

In one instance, while strolling through the streets, they looked up and noticed a man standing on a beautiful wrought-iron balcony.

"We're here with a young Canadian recording artist. Can we use your balcony?" Klovan called up.

The man agreed, and Alanis lip-synched the song from the ornate perch as Beauchamp and Howe filmed from below.

At Notre Dame, they spotted a fleet of parked limos, and Klovan sweet-talked a driver into letting them film the singer climbing out of the stretch. In another scene, Klovan appears in a cameo, licking an ice cream, part of a never-realized plan to make Alfred Hitchcock–like cameos in all her videos.

During the week of shooting, Paris was already hot. Each day, they'd walk past the École Militaire fountain, and Alanis would say she wanted to jump in and cool off. "We knew at night it lit up and looked incredible. We didn't have any permits or anything," Klovan says. But Alanis didn't let that stop her. On her last night in Paris, she decided to go swimming. Without any warning, Alanis changed into her bathing suit and headed to the fountain. Howe and Beauchamp set up the lights and camera, which drew a curious crowd. As the pre-recorded track boomed out, Alanis "just dove in and went nuts," says Klovan.

After a while, Alanis had enough and stepped out of the water. Suddenly the fountain and lights shut down. They were set on a timer and had gone off automatically — just as they wrapped the video.

The shoot had been hard work, but both Klovan and Howe believe Alanis's good nature and ease in front of the camera made things go much smoother. The film was edited back in Ottawa, and the finished product is undeniably a professional, appealing package. It also plays up the teen singer's sexuality, particularly in the swimsuit-clad fountain sequence. But Alanis says the video was not meant to exploit or objectify her; she simply wanted to jump in the fountain.

The video was sent out along with a demo cassette, which included "I'll Walk Away," "One Bad Apple," and a song called "Be Your Girl." The package got some initial interest (Howe recalls BMG was intrigued), but it quickly cooled. Coincidentally, Howe and Reny were also looking for another deal for One To One and had arranged a meeting with John Alexander of MCA Music Canada.

Formerly with the Ottawa band Octavian, Alexander was a friend of Howe's and was then working as a talent scout for MCA.

Alexander listened to the One To One material without much comment. Then, just as he was about to leave, Howe stopped him. "Before you go, I want to play you something," Howe said, and slipped the Paris video into his VCR.

Reny stared at him in disbelief, worried that Alanis's appeal could detract from One To One's chances.

Alexander was obviously impressed as he watched the video. Reny says, "I saw John's eyes going, cha-ching, cha-ching. 'I'm going to make lots of money off of this. This is the new Tiffany. She'll do anything. She's young. She's cute.'" Howe and MCA were in business.

▽

On the table in front of Heather Perkins-McVey were two contracts: the 1988 agreement Alanis and her family had signed with Howe's company, Ghettovale, and a new contract Howe had already signed with MCA. Across the desk from the lawyer sat Alanis and her parents, eager for her opinion. Should Alanis seal the deal and become a major label recording artist?

The contract was structured so that Alanis would make records under her 1988 Ghettovale agreement. Howe's company, in turn, would license the material directly to MCA, which would help pay for the making of the records and distribute and promote Alanis's material.

Perkins-McVey was a well-known criminal lawyer in Ottawa, and she had dabbled in entertainment law after being recruited to help the Ottawa band Eight Seconds get back their instruments after the gear had been seized. Frank Levin, the group's keyboardist, was working with Howe and Alanis, and he referred the Morissettes to Perkins-McVey to go over the MCA deal.

Howe had already negotiated a deal with the label to distribute Alanis's first album. Perkins-McVey recalls both Alanis and her parents were eager to sign. But she says she had serious concerns about locking the teenager into a contract that bound her to Ghettovale for up to five albums.

"The 1988 deal was a recording agreement. It was essentially a management agreement, because it covered all the management type issues," she explains. But Howe also ran Ghettovale. With Howe assuming some of the duties of a manager and running the label to which Alanis was signed, Perkins-McVey worried there could be a conflict of interest. "Obviously it was going to be in Leslie's interest. A long-term deal is in Leslie's interest, but it might not be in Alanis's interest. That was my big crusade."

She told Alanis that she was concerned about the potential for conflict of interest, and about how the deal, as it stood, gave Howe and Ghettovale too much control. She concedes that it is not unusual in the record business, especially with unproven talent, for deals to be stacked in favour of the record company or management. After all, like Howe's $100,000 gamble on Alanis, they are the ones rolling the dice with an untested artist. So there was nothing abnormal about the terms of the Ghettovale deal; however, because Howe needed Alanis to sign the licensing deal with MCA, Perkins-McVey felt the singer had leverage to reopen the 1988 Ghettovale agreement and negotiate some concessions for her own benefit.

"It was signed when she was fourteen years old. She had no rights under this agreement. Very few rights in any event," she says. "The Ghettovale Productions agreement of 1988 would not have been something I would recommend a client to sign today or back then. I would definitely change it. It was all at Ghettovale's option. She had no power."

Howe says the deal was designed to protect his investment in Alanis's career. "For me to invest all that time and money, I'm not going to do it on a handshake. It has to be a proper business thing, where, if something happens, I don't want to get the boot after two years of work," he says.

According to Perkins-McVey, the forty-page deal granted Howe and/or Ghettovale: right of first refusal as producer on Alanis's recordings; right to choose a studio (and if the studio was Distortion, it specified a rental fee of $50,000); and final decision on recording with other artists.

Ghettovale and the artist were mutually to agree on "producers, directors, creative and technical personnel," but if they disagreed, Ghettovale's decision was "final and binding." An unsigned draft of the contract also includes a provision for Ghettovale to receive 50 percent of any licensing or merchandising (T-shirts, posters, endorsements) and 10 percent of "all publishing income payable to The Artist" (meaning 10 percent of Alanis's share of their songwriting income).

By contrast, the MCA deal was less complex. Under the MCA contract, Howe was agreeing to furnish the services of Alanis. So Alanis needed to sign the contract, because, as Perkins-McVey says, the label wanted Alanis, not Howe. The lawyer believed that by changing the Ghettovale deal, the balance of power could be tipped back in Alanis's direction.

However, if it wasn't changed, Perkins-McVey advised Alanis that at the very least, under laws pertaining to the capacity of a minor to set aside a contract, she could live with the Ghettovale deal for two years, and when she turned eighteen, she could argue that she wanted out. The key to making that point was to have the contract set aside around the time she reached adulthood. Living under the terms of the contract in question once she became an adult could "imply you are consenting," she says.

Perkins-McVey advised Alanis and her family to take some time and seriously consider the long-term consequences. In fact, when it became clear she wanted Alanis and Ghettovale to revisit the 1988 deal, Perkins-McVey received faxes from Howe, eager to close the deal as it was. Howe was pushing for a quick resolution of the contract issue, and suggested that delaying or changing the original agreement could jeopardize the whole deal with MCA, Perkins-McVey says. "He wasn't too impressed with me. I don't think he would have anything nice to say about me," she comments. And she's right.

Howe recalls that she tried to get the deal substantially changed from five albums down to one, and he advised the Morissettes to get themselves a music lawyer, suggesting that Perkins-McVey was unfamiliar with typical music industry negotiations. Alanis recalls that

Perkins-McVey herself urged the Morissettes to get another opinion on the deal.

The family did, in fact, go to another lawyer, and eventually the 1988 Ghettovale contract was renegotiated after the release of the first MCA album. And while he declines to discuss the new terms of the deal, Howe says Alanis did receive "a normal artist advance, industry standard," but the five-album option Ghettovale held apparently wasn't altered.

"Obviously, we tried to get the best deal from MCA as we could," Howe says, adding that what was good for Alanis was good for Ghettovale.

During the negotiations, Alanis told *Ottawa Citizen* reporter Greg Barr she was prepared to wait for the deal to sort itself out. "I've waited so long for this, I can be patient a bit more. Now I know that it is happening, I can wait for it," she said, expressing a patience Perkins-McVey did not detect.

In the end, with the tantalizing prospect of inking a big-time record deal within reach, the threat of losing that opportunity decided the issue. Alanis and her parents listened to all the warnings, but decided that the deal was too important to jeopardize. On February 14, 1990, Alanis gave herself and Ghettovale a special Valentine gift. She closed the deal.

6

Alanis-Nadinia and New York Fries

All during the negotiations, the songwriting and packaging of Alanis continued. Even her name was called into question at this point.

According to Klovan, Howe had been concerned as far back as the Paris video shoot that there were too many one-named wonders on the charts — Tiffany, Prince, Madonna — and suggested they give Alanis a new name. Klovan disagreed, believing the days when stars had to take on bland new names was over. They considered just using her first and middle names, Alanis Nadine, but it didn't sound right. "Next we started calling her Nadinia," Klovan says, "then we started thinking of calling her Natasha. But Leslie thought, let's not go too far. So we went with Alanis-Nadinia. I was never really comfortable with it." But Alanis liked the name Alanis-Nadinia because Nadinia was her grandmother's name: "I remember being completely comfortable with using my middle name as opposed to my last name." Whatever the case, the name must have stuck for a while. Some early promotional pictures and newspaper stories identify her as Alanis-Nadinia. And Klovan prepared a bio under the Alanis-Nadinia monicker.

Ultimately, a seven-syllable name proved to be too much. When she appeared in public, no one could pronounce it correctly, and so it was dropped within six months. For the purposes of her record deal, she would become known as Alanis. Period.

Shortly before finalizing the deal with MCA, Alanis and Klovan travelled to Toronto to watch Madonna perform what turned out to be a controversial concert at SkyDome (a show immortalized in her documentary film *Truth or Dare* as police officers show up to charge her with indecency). The main purpose was to allow Alanis to meet officials at MCA; as with their sojourn to New York for *Star Search*, Klovan believes Alanis's personal contact with the label made all the difference in getting the big machine behind her record. "She just blew them away. They really had a lot of confidence in her, because she was so mature. Her charisma was so strong. All those little things added to it." A source at MCA confirms that whatever staffers thought of her music, the singer herself was always popular. Everyone wanted Alanis to do well.

As they continued working on Alanis's first album, Reny says family and friends began pointing out the uncanny resemblance between her singing style and Alanis's. But Alanis's disposition deflated any potential rivalry between the two.

"I know back then she copied me and stuff and I didn't care. I never begrudged her anything," says Reny. "I know my family and people close to me used to get real mad. 'She sounds just like you. She's trying to sing just like you.'" Had Alanis acted like a "little snotty bitch," Reny says she may have grown jealous. But the youngster was always likeable, both women had rewarding careers in music, and the two became close friends. They'd hang around the studio together and although Alanis never asked for singing tips, she did make a point of being in the studio whenever Reny recorded vocals for One To

One records. "That was her way of asking for tips. She didn't come out and say: 'Okay, so how do you sing like that?' She would just watch me."

Around this time, Alanis was given another chance to test her performing ability — this time at the 1990–91 Vocal Warz contest held at Barrymore's, a converted vaudeville hall on Ottawa's Bank Street. Sponsored by an electronics manufacturing company, Vocal Warz was designed as a talent-finding contest, pitting the best singers against one another in regional competitions.

For weeks, the elimination rounds had audiences packed into the five-hundred-seat club, and the final week of the competition had Alanis up against two other singers: Tyley Ross, who went on to play the title role in the Toronto stage production of *Tommy*, and Laury Schedler, who now works out of Toronto and recently released her own album. Schedler ended up winning with a rendition of "Papa Was a Rolling Stone." Alanis came in third.

After accepting a cheque for $1,000 and a new stereo, Schedler spotted a dejected-looking Alanis slinking away from the event. Even though she was ecstatic with her win, Schedler wanted to go up to her and say, "This means nothing." But she didn't get her chance. She was impressed by Alanis — but perhaps it was more the raw talent than the performance. "I think there were a lot of elements about Alanis that were already great at that point," says Schedler. "And I thought she was so young and singing her own song and going out there. It was very sort of put-together onstage. She would walk here, walk there. And that was sort of the way she was born and bred."

Alanis met other young musicians passing in and out of Howe's Distortion Studios. Drummer Richie Wright bumped into her while making demos at the studio with the Ottawa band Big Life (coincidentally, the group also featured Tyley Ross), and she began hanging out with him and other musicians working out of the studio. Before long, they came up with the idea of putting a cover band together. With Kevin Little on bass, Rick Kumar on guitar, Wright on drums, and Alanis on vocals, the group began rehearsing a wildly diverse set of top-forty hits — everything from Pat Benatar, Blondie, and seventies disco-funk kings Wild Cherry to Cheap Trick, Richard Marx, and the B-52s.

After some rehearsal, an agent phoned Wright at his day job at a suburban mall to say he had work for the band, but he needed a name. The players hadn't agreed on one yet, so Wright took a quick look around at the signs in the mall's food court. "There was the Teriyaki Experience and New York Fries." He chose the latter. The New York Fries (NYF on their posters), Alanis's first rock 'n' roll venture, was born.

The group performed no more than a dozen weekends during an eighteen-month stretch. At fifteen or sixteen, Alanis was younger than her bandmates (who were all around eighteen), and technically she was too young to even enter a bar, let alone take to the stage. "We never told anyone her age. And she held her own. She carried herself as a bit older," says Wright.

After one of their first gigs, in Williamsburg, Ontario, a bar patron approached the stage and began to harass Alanis. Wright was terrified by the confrontation, but he and the other band members stood up to the lout and Alanis took the incident in stride. At future shows, the New York Fries brought along a bigger friend who served as a kind of bodyguard. When they walked out into the bar, they would enter as a cluster with Alanis in the middle, out of harm's way.

While her main gig was making dance records, Wright says he could tell she had the makings of a great rock singer, even back then. "I thought she was wicked. I remember thinking at the time, 'This dance stuff is great and all, but she is singing the rock stuff really well. She seems more comfortable just letting loose.'"

The group even talked of making the New York Fries a full-time occupation if Alanis's work with Howe didn't pan out. Given the chance, Alanis may have opted to go off in a harder-edged musical direction earlier on. She may have been a fan of dance music, but when the band covered Janet Jackson's rock-flavoured song "Black Cat," her bandmates could see how eager she was to let go.

"At the time I don't think she knew what she wanted," Wright says. "She was young and when kids are young, they are impressionable

. . . She wasn't sure inside if (dance music) was what she completely wanted."

Alanis says now that she thinks it was unfortunate that she felt she had to compartmentalize her stylistic preferences. "I love music. Any kind of music. I will listen to classical, jazz, ethnic music. I love loops (the sampled drum beats used in dance music). I love rock music. And I felt I couldn't do everything at once . . . The pop sensibility was on the record. The rock guitar part was in the band."

Howe felt that the band would be a good way for Alanis to get some experience onstage. But Wright remembers that initially Howe was less enthusiastic about Alanis's venture. He recalls Howe saying that the NYF experience was making her sing like a rock singer, instead of a dance act. When Howe did attend a performance at the Talisman Hotel, he had pointed criticism for his protegée. "Sometimes I thought it was uncalled for," says Wright. "But he did it. He had invested his money and stuff in her. I don't blame him. He would critique her and it would fluster her a little."

Howe says that's taking the whole experience too seriously. It was just a fun way to get Alanis another performing outlet. "They didn't play that many gigs. It was kind of like they threw it together and rehearsed. It was a little side thing."

Alanis's stage presence did need some work, Wright concedes. Even when the band was going wild, Alanis would be glued to centre stage, "bopping" away with a smile on her face. She didn't talk to the crowd much nor did she take command of the room.

The most important thing was that New York Fries gave her a taste of things to come. "Even at that time," she now says, "I knew what the future held for me, in the sense that I would be writing music that I loved, that was exactly an extension of me, and I knew that that would result in me being in a band, and I would have to get as much experience as I could doing that."

The New York Fries may never have amounted to much, but in a way, it could have given Alanis a more natural introduction to the music business than she had been getting up until then. Signing deals, setting marketing strategies, and working through endless studio sessions at such a young age is an uncommon and arguably artificial way to make music. By contrast, meeting a group of friends with shared interests and playing together simply for the pleasure of making music, as Alanis did with New York Fries, is a much more natural way of finding an artistic footing. But Alanis's career was already set; her main job would be making records at Distortion Studios.

▽

Apart from her NYF gigs, Howe and Alanis worked late nights at the studio, coming up with material for her debut album, and Alanis had to acclimatize herself to Howe's writing method. Their songs would start with Howe working alone, creating brief passages of music he calls "riffs." Then he and Alanis would come to the studio, take the riff, and go off to separate rooms to experiment with melodies and rough lyrical ideas. Later they would get back together and play for each other what they'd come up with. The one with the best idea got their part in the song. In a way, it was like a contest to see who could come up with the best stuff.

"I guess it is a little bit overwhelming," says Reny, who has been a part of many similar sessions. "You are sort of in a competition. It's not a question of: 'I want this song on my album.' You don't have that option. In one way, it's great. It makes you work harder, and it is good to be surrounded by people who are talented and more experienced than you." If ideas get rejected, it's all in the name of making a great record, she adds.

Howe's game plan was to write the best music possible, and he didn't care who came up with the best idea, as long as good ideas made it onto tape.

"So maybe her stuff wasn't used as much. So therefore, it would be kind of discouraging . . . It probably helped her to strive for better things than 'I wrote this song when I was really depressed, and it really sucks. But it means a lot to me,'" Reny says.

But Howe's studio method did stick in the craw of keyboardist Frank

Levin, who had been invited in as a songwriter, keyboardist, and co-producer. Levin, whose work with Eight Seconds was more pop-oriented, wasn't as interested in dance music. There just wasn't enough room in the studio for both musicians' ideas, so Howe began working with keyboardist Serge Côté, leaving Levin with a reduced role. "It was too hard to work together. Nothing against the guy. I love him like a brother. He has got a heart of gold. But when it came to working in the studio, we never saw things eye-to-eye," Levin says.

With Alanis dividing her time among home, school, the studio, Klovan's schedule of appearances, and NYF gigs, she did have to delegate some of the creative process to Howe. "Obviously, I was a fairly experienced songwriter. We worked together on as much as we could," he says, adding he ended up writing the bulk of the lyrics for the first album. "It is not like she could write a whole song and give it to me." But Howe bristles at the suggestion that she was just along for the ride, responding to his cues. She may not have been completely behind every single creative decision made in the studio, but she listened to the opinions of her more experienced collaborators and the final product was a reflection of her personality and her influence.

"To say things were forced on her or she's just a robot or automaton is just ridiculous," Howe states. "She is a very, very intelligent person, probably one of the brightest people I've ever worked with. She has opinions and a personality of her own. If there was something she definitely didn't like, I wouldn't even dream of forcing it on her. She's not going to feel good about it, and it is still her career."

No one was holding a gun to Alanis's head in the studio, but she says she sensed there was another more personal, perhaps less commercial, way to write songs that never really got explored during her time at Distortion Studios. "I guess there was a voice in my head that said: 'Well, maybe I had it all wrong and this is the right way to do it.' I didn't know what integrity meant when I was younger. That's a nice sort of adult word. I didn't really understand what my gut was saying. I thought it was a little naïve. But only as I got older did I realize it was my gut I should listen to, and not anything else."

It's clear that the grooming Alanis received during those years would prepare her for a career as a pop star. What it failed to do, though, was to help her cope with the special demands and extraordinary pressure that a career would bring.

7

A Package of
Perfection

To all outward appearances, Alanis was on top of the world. She was young. She was pretty. She was talented. She had a recording career. She was becoming famous around Ottawa.

Yet as her partners finished the record, she was experiencing incredible strain, even though she managed to keep it well hidden. By day, she was enrolled at Glebe Collegiate, in the highly challenging Program for Advanced Learning classes. By night, she was writing and recording at Distortion, often until the early morning hours, and she was still maintaining a busy schedule of public appearances under Klovan's direction. Her career (and those of her collaborators) was at stake. And on top of all that, there were the usual trials of adolescence.

"I wish I could have had me as an older sister, to tell me that it was all fine, and some of the routes I was taking were self-destructive," Alanis says now. "That whole teenage era, for me, I would not replay it for a million dollars. I'm glad I went through it and it contributed to what I am as a person. But I would never want to go back to that time. And I hope one day I will be able to look back with some positive feelings, but right now, I can't. I don't have very many positive feelings about school in general."

Alanis was a perfectionist, and her own drive to achieve, coupled with the needs and expectations of those she was working with, was a heavy load for someone so young. Being aware of the demands of the entertainment industry did not make her life any easier, especially as she was always trying to meet those expectations: "I was much too concerned with other people's perception of what I was doing . . . So I would come across as this package of perfection." She was left with a constant feeling of failure. At an age where most teens are still dreaming of what their adult life will bring, she had adults whose professional and financial welfare depended on her.

Her parents were aware of the problems Alanis was dealing with. She seemed stressed and confused at times. Her father Alan was ready to step in say: "Just stop! Don't work with these people anymore." But he held back because he knew that if he came down heavy, Alanis would have left home and done it anyway. As a result, Alanis says Alan felt partly responsible for her unhappiness during that period, feeling that he didn't protect her from some of the "wolves" she may have encountered. "But I bless him for not protecting me," she says. "I have no harboured anger. I am completely at peace with it."

Alanis makes it clear, even now, that it was her call. She wanted to be in the spotlight, so she was prepared to get burned. "It was my decision. To this day, I know that that is what goes along with it. If that's what I want to do, there are certain sacrifices." So the pattern she established early on continued. She would push herself to reach the expectations she and others set. But she maintained a sunny façade that matched the upbeat outlook of her music. Making music made her happy, but it wasn't an artistic outlet for her pain.

Klovan was aware of the weight pressing down on Alanis's shoulders, and he felt obliged to watch out for her, as he had during their road trips together earlier in her career. He saw the heavy toll the late nights and performances were taking on her, but says it was all part of her development. "Without all that experience, she wouldn't be the total performer she is today. You could see the evolution and maturing of her as a performer."

High school, where her rising fame didn't go unnoticed by her peers, was another constant source of stress. Usually kids get picked on for their weaknesses, but in Alanis's case, she attracted derision because she was pretty and talented and becoming a local celebrity. Kids didn't seem shy about saying what they thought about her — even right to her face. Whether they were jealous or simply didn't like her music, they could be insulting and cruel.

"When's your stupid CD coming out," one classmate taunted.

"When's yours coming out, missy," Alanis shot back, a retort which, for a time, stifled the catty comments. But the worst of it happened behind her back, often within earshot of her twin brother, Wade, and close friends who either had to endure the sniping or defend Alanis's name. "God, it's funny. I immediately think not of what I had to tolerate, but what my brother had to tolerate," Alanis says.

But while the insults hurt, they didn't discourage her. "I knew I was doing something musical and creative and that is as pure as it was. I wasn't doing anything wrong, so if people were upset with me, it was for their own reasons."

Some teachers, as well, were opposed to what Alanis was doing and called her parents in to voice their disapproval. They presumed that she would expect to be treated differently, when all she really wanted was to be treated like anybody else. The majority of her teachers and schoolmates were supportive, however.

The jealousy Alanis encountered amongst her peers, combined with her maturity, made her run with an older crowd. Even when she entered Glebe Collegiate in grade nine, she spent time with kids closer in age to her older brother, Chad. One of those friends was Lori

Thompson, who feels that older kids were secure enough to relate to Alanis without envy: "She probably got a lot more support from people who were older, because there wasn't all that competitiveness."

With everything that was happening to her, Alanis tried to maintain a low profile. She never denied her showbiz ambitions, but her friends agree she did her best never to rub her schoolmates' noses in her success. "She was pretty discreet about it," says her friend Krysia Kehoe, "but if somebody asked her, she was willing to say: 'This is what I do.'"

Alanis may have privately struggled, but publicly, she maintained a sunny veneer. "To me anyway, she didn't volunteer a lot of information," says Kehoe. "She didn't involve too many people in that. She is very easygoing. She could have hidden anything that she didn't feel good about."

In fact, Alanis's friends were impressed with her ability to juggle her career and school work, which typically landed her on the honour role. They describe her as always running off somewhere — dance lessons, singing sessions, performances. "We were always amazed that she was able to do her schoolwork on top of that. She had such a packed schedule," says Thompson.

There was time for dating, but Alanis never became involved in long-term relationships. As in the days of *You Can't Do That on Television*, her maturity set her apart from her peers. And the low self-esteem she privately fought during this time left her with "chronic incompatibility" problems when it came to matters of the heart. "I'd date older men so I could talk to them, and then get my sexual fix with younger guys," she told *Billboard* magazine. "I was active and physically doing the things that were sexual when I was younger," she told *Rolling Stone*. "There was one side of me that was crazy and deviant, doing things ahead of my time, and another side that was very held back, wanting to remain virginal for the sake of being the good white Catholic girl." She told *Details* magazine she waited until she was nineteen to lose her virginity, but "I was very sexually active since I was fourteen, doing everything but. Isn't that odd? I enjoyed what I was doing, but I couldn't fully enjoy it." She went on say: "The only way I felt desirable was when a man would leave his girlfriend for me. I wish I could go back and apologize to all the girls I did that to."

Now she sees that the split between older and younger men was a result of spending so much time in the adult world at an early age. And she yearned to somehow bridge the gap. When she was with people her own age, the youthful, exuberant part of her would be fulfilled, but the other part would be very lonely. The opposite was true in the other situation, where she would spend a lot of time with adults and date people much older than she was. "The intellectual part of me was fulfilled with them, but the younger part, running around and stopping for ice cream and being somewhat irresponsible, was completely denied. I found myself bouncing like a pinball between those two existences." What she yearned for was a boyfriend who satisfied both her youthful and mature sides. But being unable to find that perfect match meant that she never seemed to date any one guy for long. Kehoe would tease her about how fussy and easily bored she was in relationships. "She wouldn't even bother to think of any kind of relationship. She was playing it safe."

Despite her youth, she was able to join her adult friends at the cool bars in Ottawa's Byward Market. Kehoe, who was old enough to legally enter bars, watched out for her younger friend, keeping an eye on anyone who might put a "wrong move" on Alanis. If she spotted a would-be Romeo making slick advances, Kehoe would quietly suggest Alanis return to their table. "I was kind of like the older sister at the time. I guess maybe she didn't like that all the time . . . She would say, 'Just leave me alone.'"

Lori Thompson says recent rumours about Alanis's behaviour during those early underage pub-crawls are all wrong. "I've heard all these stories about how she used to give bouncers a really hard time and flaunt her fame and act like she was some sort of VIP, even back then. I was with her at these places and I don't remember her doing any of that," she says. "It was almost like singing was a part-time job after school."

While her friends could help her deal with some of the rejection and attention at school, Alanis also had to learn to deal with professional criticism. She had been hurt by the lukewarm reception she received from record labels prior to signing with MCA. But as Klovan points out, "You have to step out of yourself as a performer and not be overly critical about rejection. It's not meant to be taken personally, but some performers do. Alanis was pretty good about it."

Howe felt the singer faced the pressure like a "trouper," able to handle the constant juggle of school and music career. "There were some stressful times, for sure. It's not always fun and easygoing. But considering this was her growing-up period, she handled it extraordinarily well — as well as anybody could be expected to at that age."

And as Alanis became better known, demands for her time kept growing. Every charity and community event in town requested her help. Something had to give, so she opted to quit New York Fries. The band had served its purpose by giving her exposure to the demands and the fun of live performance, but now she needed to focus. With a record about to be released and a career soon to shift into high gear, the demands on her time were shifting into high gear, as well.

8

Too Hot

In April 1991, MCA and Ghettovale jointly issued Alanis's first album, simply called *Alanis*. The result of months of recording and writing with Howe and the crew at Distortion, the ten tracks are spiked with hip, sampled dialogue and crammed with funky drum loops, layers of synthesizers, and a collage of vocals — a deeply danceable collection of songs.

"You can feel the fun we had writing the songs as soon as you listen," the press bio quoted Alanis. "The excitement you hear is real. Writing from noon until sometimes five in the morning, or stopping the car somewhere to jot down just that particular line in one of the lyrics . . . all of this contributed to what we wanted with the music. We wanted songs that made sense; we took real life situations, real life love affairs and real life emotions and put them into each song."

However, apart from the ballad "On My Own" ("I hope a lot of young people can relate. I put a lot of feeling into that one," she says in the bio), it's hard to imagine what influence Alanis's real life situations and emotions had to do with the songs. Howe and company had an undeniable flair for writing catchy melodies and orchestrating great radio pop. But the lyrics on *Alanis* are flyweight, escapist declarations of love, little more than an excuse to unleash her effective vocals.

MCA threw its promotional might behind her, hosting a party in Ottawa to launch the record. Alanis told the crowd she was still surprised by the realization of her dream. "It wasn't until that moment when I walked in the room and everyone was applauding that it hit home, that I'd finally done it," she told the *Ottawa Sun*'s Rick Overall. "It was such a good feeling, I still can't describe it."

Alanis, both the record and the singer, drew the expected comparisons to teen hitmakers of the day, and parallels were inevitably drawn to Tiffany and Debbie Gibson. But while those teens may have been chronological peers, Alanis's collaborators believe her music was a cut above. "We never tried to emulate them," says Klovan, "but they were so successful, we kind of used them for a guideline for what she was doing."

Howe rejects any "teenybopper" tag being tied to Alanis, dismissing Gibson and Tiffany as "wimpy, sort of bubblegum girly stuff." He saw *Alanis* as a "more streety, mature type outlook and type of music" and thought the music had another dimension that Debbie Gibson's and Tiffany's lacked.

Even unflattering comparisons couldn't hurt the CD, which became a huge success. Radio pounced on the first single, "Too Hot," which was accompanied by a flashy, sexy video. She also filmed a clip for a re-recorded version of "I'll Walk Away" (retitled "Walk Away"), which included an appearance by Matt Leblanc, later a cast member on the TV show *Friends*. "Having a little sex thrown in there is OK," she told the *Ottawa Citizen*'s Greg Barr of her videos. "But there's no way I want people seeing me and saying: 'She's only sixteen? Oh, that little slut, what is she doing?'" She also told Barr that she had been given a lot of freedom for someone so young. "I haven't met any other sixteen-year-olds who have gotten this kind of opportunity. (The record company) is letting me write and do my own dancing, whereas some girl singers are completely manufactured."

By July, "Too Hot" had edged into the contemporary hit radio top ten, nestled next to hits by EMF and Paula Abdul. In August, the singer travelled to Toronto to shoot a video for another single, "Feel Your Love," with a reported budget of $45,000. "I love Janet Jackson and Madonna, but I want Alanis to look like Alanis," she told the *Toronto Sun*.

With the album and videos, there was a new emphasis on Alanis's physical appearance. Alanis felt pressure to maintain a sleek physique and to be overly strict with her diet. "My weight has been all over the place since I was twelve," she told the *Toronto Sun*. So she began to run ten kilometres, cycle for thirty minutes, and swim every day. Klovan was concerned about Alanis and her dieting, especially since she was at an age when many young women experience eating disorders. But the dieting never got out of hand; no matter how hard she was on herself, she says her body would say no, it wasn't going to let her take it to an extreme. "Any time you deprive yourself of food or anything for the sake of what society wants you to be, your system, or the universe, is going to make sure you get even more of it than you need," she says.

She worked forty hours straight on the "Feel Your Love" video, which featured her high-stepping around shirtless, muscular hunks. The pace was gruelling, but she said she was inspired by the knowledge that this was her one and only shot. If she needed to sleep, she could wait and then go home to crash for twenty hours. But while she had the chance, she had to put every ounce of energy into her work.

▽

Alanis's first shot at performing her new music live came on August 24, 1991, when she played at the bottom of a four-act rap-dance package at Ottawa's Frank Clair Stadium — a show headlined by fleeting rap superstar Vanilla Ice, who was then riding high on the charts with the song "Ice Ice Baby."

Alanis kicked off the evening with a three-song set, including "Feel Your Love" and "Too Hot." "She proved she's got the voice and the stage presence, no problem there, all she needs is a hot band and the lady's on her way," the *Ottawa Sun*'s Rick Overall wrote the next morning.

Onstage after Alanis's brief showcase, second-billed Canadian rapper Maestro Fresh Wes had his set cut short, apparently after Vanilla Ice's crew pulled the plug. Unseen by the grandstand crowd, about a dozen crew members from both acts squared off in a punchout. Stage hands scrambled to separate the two volatile camps, and police were called in to maintain order backstage.

Alanis was oblivious to the brawl. She was in her dressing room signing autographs for kids, relishing the moment. "I remember being really excited . . . This was an outdoor show where it was light out, and I could see everyone," she recalls.

Alanis also performed a six-song set opening for the dance outfit C&C Music Factory in the Toronto area, but most of her work supporting the album was done through a cross-country promotional tour. "There was nobody else like her in Canada, so she really clicked into the right place at the right time," Klovan says. "There was obviously a big void for a performer of her style and calibre. Because she was so personable on these promotional tours, everybody just fell in love with her; the radio people were only too happy to promote the heck out of her."

Everyone was amazed that the album did so well, so quickly. The success of *Alanis* even caught Alanis by surprise. But she did not permit herself the luxury of revelling in her success. "At the time, I kept walking that line of humility and selling myself short, compensating for what I thought was going to be too much attention, which would result in other people being jealous. So at all costs, ward off the attention."

▽

As momentum for the debut album built, MCA's John Alexander began to take an increasingly important role in Alanis's career.

The album went gold within three months of its May 1991 release — something MCA didn't expect in the recessionary marketplace at the time — and he and Alanis spent the summer criss-crossing the country, doing "grip-and-grins" (quick meetings, often combined with photo opportunities) with record retailers, radio DJs, and music critics. Along the way, Alexander and Alanis forged a lasting personal and professional relationship. He provided a consistent, stable base for Alanis, and his low-key approach to crises had a welcome calming effect on Alanis and her collaborators.

After Alanis's early success, Alexander's career continued to grow. First he moved to New York, then Los Angeles, where up until early 1997, he worked as an executive with MCA Music Publishing, the company that still administers Alanis's songs. But despite scaling the heights of the music biz, Alexander remained down to earth.

"I have never seen him caught up in the whole façade of it," says Klovan. "What he does is strictly business, putting money into it and taking risks. Naturally, he is very cautious. He and Alanis have a relationship that is amazing. As he has grown, he has taken her with him."

For a time, Klovan and Alexander were "doubling," both trying to manage her career at the same time. But with the record taking off and her new life demanding experienced, full-time guidance, Klovan realized he needed to step aside and let Alexander guide her. "I would never, ever, have wanted to do anything that would hold Alanis back, so that's when I pulled back a little bit."

Public appearances continued to be a big part of her workload, though, and Ottawa radio station Energy 1200, which had helped her out financially with the Paris video shoot, played her songs and put her to work at publicity events. And so Alanis agreed to do things like showing up for the morning shift to work a McDonald's drive-thru window for a charity fundraiser. Len Hanes, who was the station's promotions director at the time, remembers that Alanis would happily show up at 7 a.m. looking great and acting infectiously perky. "She was always so eager. She would talk to the people and bring them in."

As the CD took off, MCA organized an autograph session at Carlingwood, a suburban shopping mall in Ottawa. Alanis and Alexander went for coffee prior to the meet-and-greet, and as they looked across the parking lot, she noticed hundreds of people entering the mall and wondered what all the fuss was about. When she walked out to meet her fans, she found thousands of people crowded into the mall, eager to meet the singer and get her autograph. "This is really special to me because it is Ottawa and seeing you all here just makes me want to cry. This is great," she told the crowd.

Later that summer, Klovan organized a football half-time show that featured Alanis. Dancers were flown up from Toronto for the extravaganza. She performed "Too Hot" at centre field for thousands of Ottawa Rough Rider fans, accompanied by her dancers and cheerleaders.

After the song was over, Alanis was asked to remain out on the field, allegedly to draw a prize for a contest winner. Instead, Alexander and MCA president Ross Reynolds tromped across the artificial turf at Frank Clair Stadium and surprised Alanis with a gold album award, signifying sales of, at that point, 50,000 units. Television footage shot backstage after the presentation caught Alanis's reaction: "I was ready to pull the name of some winner, and the winner was me, man!"

▽

With the success of her singles and videos, the next goal was a Juno, Canada's equivalent to the Grammy awards. Winning one of the statues is always especially tough for a new act, but Alanis's CD was on its way to platinum status, and her friends in the record industry were confident she would be recognized. When the nominees were finally announced, the results were shocking. Alanis was nominated in three categories: single of the year, most promising female, and best dance record. It was a rare feat for a singer without a track record of success.

She travelled to Toronto in March 1992 for the ceremonies, and even agreed to report on the hubbub and hype surrounding the show for the *Ottawa Sun.* "I guess if I just pretend the whole thing is no big deal, I won't get nervous," she wrote in a special "postcard from the Junos" published in the paper. "Who am I kidding? This is the biggest deal ever. I love it!"

She was nervous, but there was little time to dwell on it. She had a packed schedule of interviews and appearances leading up to the ceremony, including a celebrity bowling tournament, a music industry seminar, and a guest spot on the MuchMusic dance party Electric Circus.

To add to her unease, she was panicking about her role as a presenter on the Juno telecast. Like the Grammys, the Junos are given out by the record industry to recognize excellence in music. But unlike the American ceremony, which draws from a much larger industry divided between two major music centres, New York and Los Angeles, the Canadian awards are much more insular. Although recent years have seen more independent labels spring up across Canada, the overwhelming majority of record companies and recording artists are based in Toronto. With the same colony of music-makers drawn together week after week by industry functions and year after year by the awards, the Junos have always been more intimate and relaxed than the Grammys, but no less fiercely contested.

The 1992 Juno ceremony was held at the O'Keefe Centre, a stage typically used for touring theatrical productions or upmarket musical performances. The music industry's best and brightest squeezed into the steeply stacked narrow rows of seats, typically taking one of three approaches to attire: dress up, dress down, or dress weird. Tuxedos and old T-shirts are both acceptable Juno attire. (Singer k.d. lang picked up her 1985 most promising female vocalist award in a wedding dress.) Alanis took the first option, wearing a striking off-the-shoulder creation she helped design. Inside, she may have been a bundle of nerves, but she cut a stunning figure that night. Songwriter and recording artist Tim Thorney was seated near Alanis at the awards, and he describes her that evening as "the heart of looking beautiful."

"A guy wouldn't forget that girl," says Thorney, who, within a couple of years, would become one of Alanis's closest friends.

There were performances by Bryan Adams, Tom Cochrane, and Crash Test Dummies, comedy by host Rick Moranis, and a Hall of Fame induction tribute to Ian and Sylvia Tyson. It all went by in a blur for Alanis. Suddenly, someone was onstage tearing open an envelope and reading her name. She was the most promising female vocalist of the year.

She made it to the stage in a daze, managed to utter an acceptance speech, and was led off to the press area. Photos taken moments after she accepted the award caught her with a look of glee and disbelief frozen on her face. "I think it was pretty obvious I was overwhelmed that night," Alanis says.

Klovan, who was at the show, says winning the Juno was the "icing on the cake."

"It was an acknowledgement," he says. "I don't know if Alanis was convinced. It seemed too good to be true for her."

As she clutched the Juno in one hand and faced the popping flash-bulbs, all the disappointments and sacrifice faded away. This was Alanis's moment.

9

A Reality Check

The biggest problem with success is trying to follow it. With such an outstanding debut came increased expectations. Alanis and her team had a big job ahead of them.

During the time off between the platinum-plus triumph of *Alanis* and work on her next album, Alanis had to go through the awkwardness of returning to regular school life. Imagine appearing on national television one night as the toast of the Canadian music industry. Then imagine trying to slip inconspicuously back into algebra class on Monday, without making your peers jealous.

"Some people were cool about it," says Alanis. "Some people didn't care about it. And some people were really upset by it and would do anything to make you feel horrible."

On top of that, normal life couldn't help but seem anti-climactic.

As a perfectionist who strived so hard to achieve, the rewards left Alanis unsatisfied and a little frustrated. "Society leads you to believe that if you achieve this success, whether it is winning awards or selling millions of records, everything is great and you get approval from people . . . And then you achieve it and nothing is different."

She never complained, but friends say resentment among her schoolmates was inadvertently fuelled by the school's decision to play her version of "O Canada" over the PA system daily. Playing the song once would have been a nice novelty. Repeating her "O Canada" every day gave her detractors a daily anti-Alanis ritual.

"If they don't want to hear it, it's one thing. But the extent they went to to show they didn't want to hear it was ridiculous," Alanis says, adding that some people didn't hesitate to express their dislike of her singing right to her face. For someone who was trying to downplay her success, trying to fit in at school and not draw attention to herself, hearing morning announcements became a daily agony.

Louise Reny was sympathetic. She says there can be little doubt the anthem was the source of much animosity. "You just know you are not going to have many girlfriends. You know all the chicks are going to be totally jealous of you."

In a strange way, school becomes the "totally surreal" experience for a young performer and the record business side becomes a lark, says Reny. "The music stuff is fun. The record company is fun. Even when you are not young, it is still fun. You get taken out to dinner . . . You get to go backstage. That part is way more of a breeze than the high school part. The reality is going to school Monday morning and facing these people and some of them are just backstabbing. To your face, they are all nice to you, but behind your back . . ."

While she was working through her last couple of years of school in the real world, Alanis grabbed two chances to portray school life on screen. In June 1992, she hosted the docudrama *Borderline High*, a YTV special aimed at high school dropouts. She also flew out to Vancouver to film scenes for a little-seen Corey Haim film, variously known as *Boys Will Be Girls, Just One of the Girls*, or *Anything for Love*.

Haim plays a high school kid who avoids school bullies by dressing as a girl. In his music class, he composes songs as a girl (the tracks were actually Alanis's), and Alanis appears briefly in the film's high school dance finale.

Her music also made a brief appearance in a John Ritter *Problem Child* movie. One of Alanis's songs was supposed to be featured prominently in the movie, Stephan Klovan recalls, but Alanis, her family, and Klovan were disappointed when the song's profile was limited to a brief scene when Ritter walks into a diner. For about five seconds, her song could be heard in the background; if you weren't listening for it, it would easily pass unheard.

▽

Alanis's increasing renown was attracting the notice of fans of all ages, including many young men. In 1992 she began a working relationship with Ottawa's new professional hockey team, the Senators, which joined the NHL that year. When the franchise hired a train to haul hockey fans to Montreal for the amateur draft, Alanis was hired to entertain the crowd onboard. And at their nationally televised inaugural home game at the Civic Centre, the splashy opening ceremonies included a rendition of "O Canada" sung by Alanis.

One of the people she impressed was Senators player Mike Peluso. "It was just stunning. Incredible. She was gorgeous," he told the syndicated tabloid TV show *American Journal.* Peluso (who has since gone on to play for other NHL teams) was the new franchise's designated enforcer — in charge of maintaining an intimidating physical presence and punching out opposition bullies in the name of protecting his more timid teammates. With long hair trailing out from under his helmet and a fiery competitive spirit, Peluso quickly became a fan favourite. And he quickly became a fan of Alanis Morissette.

Peluso told *American Journal* that his girlfriend was out of town around the time of the opening game and that he did not hide his affection for the teen singer. "It was more along the lines of being flirtatious and hanging out. But vibes were there. We got the opportunity to spend some good, quality time together. We became pretty good friends." When his steady returned to town, though, Peluso pulled back. He told the TV show he now believes he could have handled the situation better. "I was scared. I would have done it maybe a lot different if I had to do it all over again." Peluso's encounters with Alanis obviously made a big impression on him, but the same apparently can't be said for Alanis. Friends can't recall her ever talking about him.

Alanis's work with the Senators during the 1992 hockey season got her invited to sing "O Canada" at the NHL all-star game in Montreal. But it wasn't a hockey player who was captivated with her that night. It was actor-comedian Dave Coulier.

A long-time hockey fan (he plays on a celebrity hockey team at charity events), Coulier played Joey on the TV show *Full House*, and later became host of the program *America's Funniest People*. Alanis and Coulier quickly became an item.

Their relationship "raised a few eyebrows," says Klovan. Some people remarked upon the age difference (Coulier is about fifteen years older), but it's not surprising that he would be attracted to Alanis. As far back as her nightclub sorties with Klovan, she had been attracting older men. And Alanis had said that she yearned for a boyfriend who could appeal to both her mature, thoughtful side and her carefree, teenaged side. Coulier was older, but his zany sense of humour (his comedic specialty is imitating cartoon characters) gave him the mix of experience and exuberance she sought in one man.

Coulier became Alanis's first serious boyfriend — she described him to one friend as "the love of my life." Once Klovan met Coulier, he could see that Coulier's personality meshed quite well with Alanis's, and that they seemed to have a good relationship "while it lasted," observing that there was "a great chemistry between them." The age difference never seemed to be an issue.

Early into their relationship, Coulier, who is also a qualified pilot, flew his own jet from his home in Los Angeles to Ottawa to meet Alanis's family and friends. Joining the actor on the trip was his young son from a previous relationship. Klovan couldn't resist enlisting the tot in a prank, and whispered to him: "Go over and grab Alanis's leg and say: 'Mommy, Mommy! I have to go to the washroom.'" The kid did as instructed and a flustered Alanis gave Klovan a playful hit.

Because Coulier's career kept him busy in Los Angeles, they had to be content with a long-distance relationship. But Alanis believes that living without her boyfriend for long stretches was good for her. "I was just learning how to be a responsible adult. That part of me that was really young needed to grow up," she says. Alanis felt that she needed to gain confidence and independence, and while having the support and guidance of an older boyfriend close at hand would have made the process easier, it wouldn't have been as rewarding.

Coulier and Alanis have been tight-lipped about their relationship. His comments on their time together have been limited to a few lines in a *People* magazine year-end spotlight on the singer. "She has a great sense of humor . . . She's very introspective, but at the same time a bright and happy person."

▽

Learning how to be a responsible adult meant that Alanis would have to start pushing herself artistically. Working at Howe's Distortion Studios, she ploughed into a follow-up record, working to take her music in a new direction. She didn't want this album to be as "dancey" as the first one, wishing to move beyond her "dance queen" image. She wanted to write more serious songs, which was just fine with Howe.

Howe and Alanis worked with keyboardist Serge Côté for six to eight months to create the new record at Distortion, which Howe had moved from the basement of his home to an industrial park on the outskirts of Ottawa.

In the meantime, the stress of trying to mature as an artist while following up her hit debut, as well as handling the demands of her modest celebrity and keeping on top of life at school finally got to Alanis. She suffered a kind of breakdown, and tearfully "freaked out" in her family's living room as her parents were about to leave on a trip. For the first time, the veneer of perfection began to crack.

Alanis had been keeping up a façade of complete self-confidence and strength, not showing her parents the extent of the confusion she felt inside. The stress of repressing her true feelings led to the emotional episode. "From the time I was 10," she told *Rolling Stone* magazine, "I was working with all these people trying to control me and tell me what they thought I should be and what I should look like. And I tried to control myself to be what they wanted me to be."

Alan and Georgia cancelled their trip and they helped her through the crisis by talking about the problems and assuring their daughter they were there to support her. Alanis also made the decision to undergo therapy, a process she soon came to like and would draw a lot of strength from. "Therapy became like a drug to me. I became almost as addicted to that as I was to music," she says. She read books on the subject and became fascinated by the idea of becoming psychologically aware and gaining insight into her personality and the psyches of people she met.

Alanis's breakdown took everyone by surprise — including her music partners. Leslie Howe was unaware of the extent of her troubles, and for most of that period was oblivious to her private problems. "I knew all wasn't well, but she always was optimistic. She always did her job, she did great in school. She keeps a lot of stuff inside. She was not terribly good at releasing it."

Alanis's inability to express her true feelings fuelled a simmering resentment, and therapy helped her realize that she needed to be a lot more proactive regarding her career. "I think the whole way that I was in the past was a passive–aggressive thing, where I would just sit there quietly and listen to a whole lot of things I didn't necessarily believe in, and work in environments that were really negative and difficult," she says.

In addition to analysis, her writing was becoming a therapeutic outlet of its own. Outside the studio she was still writing poems and loved the release they provided her: "When I was writing them, I was flying.

I was free." She tried to incorporate some of the free-form expression she was developing in her poetry into her songwriting, but most of this material didn't make the cut for her second album. Somewhat frustrated with the writing process, she began to ask other songwriters how their collaborations worked, both creatively and financially, and then took some new ideas back to the studio. Alanis felt that the way she and Howe had written songs when she was younger was too mechanical, that there must be an easier way than ripping "the poor song apart in order to figure out who got what."

Rather than blaming others for her problems, she now criticizes herself for not having the nerve during that period to stand up for her creative desires. She believes that had she possessed the strength to assert her ideas, her partners would have cooperated. "I take almost full responsibility for it. A lot of people thought it was a Svengali kind of thing back then. But it wasn't," she says. "For me to say, 'I wanted to do all these things and Leslie wouldn't let me,' would be an out-and-out lie. I did not feel, for the most part, repressed, when it came to how I was being portrayed . . . I wasn't judging his way. I just knew that it wasn't gelling with me very well."

Howe now acknowledges he could have been more sensitive, but felt that he didn't know the extent to which it was bothering Alanis. When they were working in the studio, Alanis would greet many of his ideas with enthusiasm, but he realizes now that she was unhappy. "Obviously, I am going with what I think is best. But I think, perhaps underneath she was thinking: 'This isn't really what I want to do, or you're not considering my ideas enough.'"

Alanis's long-standing eagerness to please had certainly helped her achieve as much as she did in her career, but it had also obviously backfired on her personally. By attempting to make everyone else happy, she had made herself miserable, and she knew that she wasn't attaining the depth of expression she wanted and needed.

▽

In the fall of 1992, MCA issued *Now Is the Time*, which Alanis hoped would be a showcase for more personal music. "This time I wanted to prove I could actually write the songs. More than anything, I wanted to prove it to myself . . . I just wanted to bare my soul in the songs," she told the *Ottawa Sun*'s Rick Overall when the record was released. "I had a lot more to do on the writing end and I feel a lot more of my own personality and feeling have come out with the music this time . . . It's much more personal because the first album was a bit of an experiment."

Despite Alanis's assertion of playing a bigger role in the songwriting, Howe says he tailored the words on *Now Is the Time* to fit her ideas. Everything had to meet with her approval, but in the end, he says most of the words she sang were his. "Don't get me wrong. It was about her, for her, and I consulted with her . . . We definitely worked on it together. But most of the lyrics were written by me or I was very heavily involved. But it was very much a collaborative effort."

Alanis was still emotionally fragile and at the record release party at a bar in the Byward Market she broke down crying during her remarks to the music industry crowd. "Even after a whole year of this, I think to myself: 'Is this really happening to me?'" she told Overall at the party. "When I think about how well the first album did, I'm really thankful, because I know so many other people in the business struggled to get their careers off the ground."

Interestingly, the CD sleeve contains a rambling, free-form piece of prose that reads like a power-of-positive-thinking treatise. "No regrets. Growth. Give yourself credit. Everybody is different. Their view of you may not be correct. Does it really matter? Who matters? . . . Conquer a fear. Don't be perfect, be excellent. Falter. Balance. Be grateful. Be real. Never give up. Don't be afraid. I believe in you."

At the time, it must have seemed that the self-assured teen was attempting to share life lessons with her listeners. But knowing the emotional turmoil she now says she was privately living with, the piece reads much more like a self-administered pep talk. And so do some of the song lyrics. "The Time of Your Life" describes her frustration at the antagonistic and patronizing attitudes she encountered. The presciently titled "(Change Is) Never a Waste of Time" describes someone who keeps her true feelings hidden behind a smile. Clearly *Now Is the Time* did manage to reflect a bit more of her personality. "I am so proud of the step between the first and the second record," Alanis says now. "I am as proud of that step between the first and second record as I am from the second to the third record (*Jagged Little Pill*)."

With Howe, she jetted off to Rome to film a video for the single, "An Emotion Away," which leaped onto the charts ahead of tracks by Bon Jovi, U2, and Canada's most popular domestic act, The Tragically Hip. The song is the most memorable of the album's ten cuts, as it was the most fully realized attempt to meld a more personal style of music with pop. *Now Is the Time* went on to sell reasonably well, but in the wake of the debut's success, sales were modest, and in the record business, too often that is considered failure. In a sense, "now" might not have been the time for another Alanis Morissette record.

Opinions on why the record failed vary. Howe wonders if it didn't suffer by attempting to bridge two different styles of music. "In hindsight, I think we were in the middle of the road. We fell halfway between pop and dance," says Howe. "If I could have done things differently, I would have gone more in the dance direction for that album." But Klovan thinks *Now Is the Time* failed by being too similar to the first album: "It wasn't different enough that people sat up and noticed it," he says. Alanis doesn't like to dwell on the record's commercial difficulties, but suspects some record buyers had trouble accommodating her stylistic change. "When certain people get to know you as one identity, they don't want you to change, because there is a comfort in having that relationship with that artist . . . I was just moving in a direction I wanted to, and was less concerned with the approval of others when I was writing it," she says. "Or it might be that people just hated the songs. And that's cool, too."

Now Is the Time truly did showcase more depth and let Alanis's underestimated voice come to the fore. But where *Alanis* was a strong dance album, *Now Is the Time* wasn't quite as accomplished at moving her dance music to a more personal place. While all those factors may have played a role in the commercial failure of *Now Is the Time*, it is more likely that the seeds of the record's downfall were sown just months after the release of Alanis's debut album. On September 10, 1991, a trio from the U.S. Pacific Northwest, unheralded outside independent music circles, released the first single from their major label debut. The song was "Smells Like Teen Spirit." The group, Nirvana. And the musical fad they unintentionally triggered was grunge.

Scruffy, loud, unpolished, and angry, grunge was so far from Alanis's perky, upbeat, slick outlook, the two seemed unable to coexist. Practically overnight, radio and record companies rewrote the rules, effectively clearing the deck for some of the pop icons of the day and spelling commercial death for many. Only well-established, well-financed, well-promoted acts survived, such as Mariah Carey and Whitney Houston. Others simply vanished.

"That just blew away the music business back then," says Howe, adding that the alternative rock revolution battered his own career. The third One To One album had been released in February 1992 to widespread indifference. Had the album been released the summer before, it would have been a hit, according to Howe. "But pop started dying just as our album was released."

After an initial warm reception, *Now Is the Time* went cold, and Alanis had to handle audience rejection so soon after tasting such great success. MuchMusic, the Canadian video channel that had given such a strong initial boost to Alanis's career, rejected a video subsequent to "An Emotion Away," Howe says.

And despite the impressive combined sales (estimated at somewhere between 150,000 and 200,000 units), Alanis's career had not been lucrative for the singer. Howe says the only payment he received for his work was in the form of recording budgets — the money Ghettovale was paid to make the Alanis albums. That left them "heavily in debt" to the record company, and they never received royalties on sales.

With blinding speed, all four wheels had come flying off Alanis's career. She and Howe mutually agreed it was time to move on. "At that point, I was disappointed," says Howe. "The music scene was changing. She wanted to write with other people and spread her wings. I wanted to concentrate on my career." But the issue of the three remaining albums Alanis owed Ghettovale on her five-album contract remained unresolved.

It would be easy to look back at this period and find fault with Alanis's collaborators. But the fact is they accomplished a tremendous amount with limited resources. They took an unknown, untested pre-teen and for a short time made for her a viable, bestselling artist. And they did it against considerable odds. Where they failed, though, was in helping Alanis discover her own voice and letting her develop a personal style that wasn't solely defined by the charting music of the day. Now, to find out what kind of artist she could become, she would have to start all over again on her own.

Two

YOU
LEARN

*"I think I've had a real life. I think
I have had a large amount of
happiness and luck and fortune.
And I've also had a lot of pain and
difficulties, as anyone has."*
— ALANIS MORISSETTE

10

Change

In March 1993, while covering the Juno Awards in Toronto, *Ottawa Sun* reporter Rick Overall bumped into Alanis at a music industry party. She had been keeping a low profile in the wake of *Now Is the Time*, and the two had some catching up to do.

Alanis was getting ready to finish high school and was considering post-secondary education — she had been accepted in psychology and communications at the University of Toronto and both her home-town schools, Carleton University and the University of Ottawa. But she hadn't given up on music and was considering putting a band together and getting out to perform "as raw as we can" by summertime.

Overall noticed that Alanis was excited about something — she nervously jumped from subject to subject and seemed dying to tell him about it. Finally, she revealed the next big step in her career. "It's not a done deal yet, but it looks as though I'll be signing with the same management firm that handles Paula Abdul," she confided. "We're taking this one step at a time. I'll be writing with a few new people and getting other ideas into the music."

The management firm she had been talking with was Atlas/Third Rail, a Los Angeles–based company jointly run by Bob Cavallo (who had guided Prince's career through the challenging-but-rewarding *Purple Rain* years) and Scott Welch. A former road manager and sound engineer, Welch had, by the nineties, earned a reputation as a skilled manager by transforming the career of Paula Abdul, a former Los Angeles Lakers cheerleader, into a bestselling dance act.

Because of Welch's work with Abdul, John Alexander had approached him about trying to secure an American release for Alanis's two Canadian albums, hoping that he could work similar magic with her career. Because Alanis seemed to have run out of steam in Canada, tapping into the mammoth U.S. market seemed the only viable option.

Welch listened to *Alanis* and *Now Is the Time* and thought she had an "amazing" voice. He was scheduled to be in New York in early 1993 and would meet with Alanis there.

"I had dinner with her, and I was just knocked out by her," Welch says. Like so many others who had had personal contact with Alanis, the manager was immediately won over. Whatever her talents as a singer and songwriter, Welch felt there was chemistry between them.

Welch and Cavallo's combined experience gave them a specific philosophy when it came to selecting clients. They have turned down lucrative opportunities to work with big names, and instead have chosen to build up a client roster of stable personalities. No screaming matches. No bailing clients out of jail at three in the morning. Just good people. During the following weeks, as Welch and Alanis had a number of long-distance conversations, he grew to like the person he was getting to know over the phone. "It is much easier to manage someone who has their own sense of where they are going," he says.

"You just try to help them get there. If you look at the artists who are really successful, that's how they are . . . I just knew I wanted to work with her."

Just over a month after Alanis spoke to Rick Overall, MCA issued a press release confirming the pact between Alanis and Atlas/Third Rail. Welch saw great promise, but believed Alanis needed to wipe the slate clean. That meant leaving the first two albums behind, and starting fresh with new songwriting partners in a new city. It was perhaps the most significant decision Welch would make regarding her career. Abandoning any notion of finding a niche in the American market for her two Canadian albums and replicating Abdul's success, he instead chose to concentrate on Alanis herself, exploring her potential. He liked the Ghettovale/MCA albums, and describes them as "great pop records," but felt it was crucial for Alanis to find new collaborators. Pairing up with new people would bring a "different dynamic" and a "different spark."

Alanis was no longer a fifteen-year-old pop singer. She was a young woman with her own sensibilities. And she wholeheartedly agreed with Welch's view of her MCA albums. "I didn't want to release those records anywhere. There were opportunities to license them in Europe or per- haps in the United States. We semi-sought after a deal in America, but really, in my gut, I did not want to do that," she says. "I wanted to release my third record as my first record anywhere else."

The first step in bringing out her own sensibilities was relocating to Toronto — a place where Alanis could learn some life lessons, because "that's what people write from," Welch says. The move was made possible through modest financial support from John Alexander and MCA Publishing. Alanis ditched her university plans. Instead, her post- secondary experience would be moving to Canada's largest city, setting up in a cheap apartment, getting by on macaroni and cheese, and enrolling in a crash course in songwriting and living on her own.

▽

In June 1993 Alanis's grandmother, aunt, and family friend Jacqui Morgan helped her turn a modest, second-floor, one-bedroom apartment into a home. Morgan hung an old set of her lace curtains in the window, which looked out over Kingston Road, a four-lane major artery with streetcar tracks embedded in the pavement. A few houses down from Alanis's new place, Kingston Road meets Queen Street East, forming the western boundary of the area called The Beach. But really, Alanis's new neighbourhood was a world apart from the gentrified homes, restaurants, and yuppie shops that the area is known for. At Alanis's end of the road, it was all doughnut and submarine sandwich shops, Kentucky Fried Chicken and a forlorn-looking Days Inn. Also nearby is the century-old Greenwood Race Track. The horses are long gone. Now the grandstand looks onto mountains of landfill, awaiting urban renewal.

It wasn't fancy, but it was just what Alanis needed. "It was very much a working space for her. I don't think she cared as much about decorating the walls as she did about music," says Jacqui Morgan, who was by then divorced from Lindsay and living in Oshawa, just east of Toronto.

Moving to Toronto meant leaving the security of family and friends, and Alanis had a difficult time adjusting. It was a big step. Compounding her unhappiness, she and Coulier split up shortly after the move, too. She kept a picture of him on her "wall of fame," a collage of photos of friends, but when a friend asked her what led to the break-up, she would only say, "I was nineteen and I wasn't ready to be a mother."

As it happened, Richie Wright, her friend from New York Fries, was in Toronto and getting over a relationship himself, and the two of them commiserated over a box of doughnuts and a rented movie. "We were both miserable people at the time," says Wright.

During this forlorn period, Alanis spent a lot of time by herself, often wandering down to the nearby beach and sitting on the same rock, staring out at the lake, wondering about the course her life had taken. Jacqui Morgan kept in touch — mostly by phone, but occasionally she came to Toronto to see Alanis, and when she did, Alanis would sometimes have tears in her eyes. Alanis also continued seeing a therapist, going about once a week. Moving to Toronto was a rough transition, but a very necessary one. As Alanis says now: "I learned that life did not owe me anything. Any dreg of victim consciousness flew out the window . . . I knew that being alone was going to kill me or be good for me."

Despite these emotional setbacks, the whole point of relocating to Toronto was to help her develop as a songwriter. And she threw herself into the work with gusto, knowing that her new manager, Scott Welch, and John Alexander were there to support her.

To help her network with other composers, Alexander and Welch arranged for Alanis to join the Songworks group, an organization of musicians that met in the offices of Peer Music in Toronto. The group — usually about fifteen participants — got together on an irregular basis, at the instigation of Peer's David Baxter. All the participants would draw a number from a hat, and those with matched numbers would pair up. (Included among the initial group of songwriters Alanis met with were the eccentric Jaymz Bee, who would later go on to record a lounge version of Alanis's "You Oughta Know," and singer Wendy Lands, who would later release her own CD, which would draw some unflattering comparisons to *Jagged Little Pill*.) In return for setting up the partnerships, Peer Music would receive a publishing percentage of whatever music came out of the sessions, although the players were free to meet up outside the workshop and write on their own. Songworks was simply a way for songwriters to network and collaborate in an easygoing, open atmosphere.

Steve Haflidson, a singer-songwriter with a strong country element in his music, drew Alanis's name at that first session. He knew little about her early music beyond what he had seen in videos, but admired her poise and presence. Although Alanis had been part of many songwriting sessions over the years, pairing up with someone on the basis of a lottery was a new and strange experience. Haflidson broke the ice by playing her "three or four melodic ideas." She zeroed in on a delicate ballad, and the two of them worked up lyrics together. It took about three sessions — one at her place and a couple more at Haflidson's home — before they came up with a finished song, called "Gone."

They debuted the song at a songwriting showcase at the Queen Street bar Ultrasound. Haflidson played guitar and Alanis sang. The song touches on themes of loss with the lyrics describing a lonely girl painted by the "colour of pain," her tears failing to convince her lover to stay, and condemned to live in a happier past. Perhaps the song was inspired by the experience of watching her own romantic or professional prospects fade, but whatever the source, Alanis delivered the lyrics with uncommon feeling, in a much more emotional way of delivering a song than she had ever given before.

The audience responded enthusiastically, cheering and clapping in the smoke-filled bar. Alanis stood grinning onstage, relishing the buzz of performing before an appreciative audience. Before the applause for their performance had died down, David Baxter from Peer Music grabbed the mike. "If there's anybody out there from MCA and her option comes up . . . ," he hinted. "You wanna know about songs and how to sing them?"

Buoyed by the success of their collaboration on "Gone," Alanis and Haflidson agreed to meet again to see if the musical sparks would keep on flying. Haflidson was impressed by her attitude — she was always smiling and had a solid work ethic, with little pretension and total commitment to the creative process, he says.

Haflidson says she seemed game to try any new style of music; "Gone" would hardly qualify as hillbilly music, but it does have a country or folk flavour that isn't present in Alanis's other work. "She just went on to other things naturally . . . It was pretty clear she had to do something different," he says.

Haflidson had his own career ambitions, but always assumed their collaborations were to be tailored for Alanis's proposed third record (although he has since recorded a version of "Gone" for his own album, and Peer Music later arranged for "Gone" to be covered by a Swedish group called Cube). "There was always the sense that this was an opportunity to have my song covered and released by a record label," he says. When they got together, they'd usually sit in Haflidson's sunny music room, with his keyboards, guitars, and recording set-up. He would play guitar or piano, and she would sit across from him and sing along, improvising melodies and lyrical ideas. Even though Alanis never came in with prepared material, lyrics and melodies flowed easily from her. Haflidson says her natural songwriting talent defies the stereotype of a woman being the "out-front" partner in a collaboration, leaning heavily on her male collaborator. "She has a real gift that way . . . She would work at a pretty quick pace. There wasn't time for a backlog of ideas."

He has a tape of the two of them in his music room, Haflidson delicately picking out the guitar melody of a song called "If I Should Be with You" and Alanis trying out vocal melodies and improvising words about feeling hesitant to open up and needing to be on her own to find herself. When their ideas run out of steam, Alanis can be heard on the tape saying a groggy but playful "thank-you, good night," which Haflidson says epitomizes her personality while working.

"She was a lot of fun to work with," he says. And he points out that the sexual frankness people found so shocking when it appeared on *Jagged Little Pill* had been working its way into her lyrics even back then, when she took particular delight in writing a suggestive line about taking her lover "deep inside."

Their third collaboration, "Taking Back the Night," saw their two styles — Haflidson's more traditional, structured style and Alanis's developing free-form method — clashing ever so slightly. He wanted the song to tell a coherent story, while Alanis favoured an abstract approach that was much more personal, if somewhat difficult to grasp. It was a return to the free-form compositional style she had attempted in her poems but had never managed to incorporate into her songwriting. At one point, Haflidson had to take a break and clear his head, "because I couldn't understand where she was coming from."

Haflidson lifted the idea for "Taking Back the Night" from the name used for the annual women-against-violence march held in many big cities every winter. "I thought: Wow, she should sing that song.

It would be so amazing. She could really connect." Even while she and Haflidson were working on the follow-ups to "Gone," Alanis was busy networking with other songwriters. She didn't wait for the Songworks lottery system, but approached participants directly, setting up writing dates at a dizzying pace. In fact, her schedule of collaborations became so packed, she'd forget exactly which song went with which writer. "I think she had trouble keeping track of all the different songs. She would show up and say: 'Okay, where were we?'" says Haflidson.

According to publishing records, Alanis quickly built a large pool of partners and songs: "Anyway" was written with writer David Charles Pickell; "Come Into Her Own" with Dean McTaggart; "Fading" and "My Cathedral" with Gordon Paul Howard; "Last Time" with Danny Leblanc; "My Last Tear" and "That'd Be Nice" with Peer Music's David Baxter; and "One Thing I Forgot" with Eddie Schwartz. She was going through titles and collaborators in a flurry. Alanis estimates that by the time she left Toronto she had written with about one hundred different collaborators and had completed about eighty songs.

One partnership would naturally lead to another. After writing a song called "Souvenirs" with singer Amy Sky, Alanis linked up with Sky's friend, guitarist, and producer Anthony Vanderburgh. Vanderburgh says there was no discussion about what direction she wanted to take with her new music. "I did not judge her by her past work. When someone comes in the door, it is a kind of challenge: Hey, let's see if we can come up with something really great. We were both pretty genuinely excited about the stuff we were writing."

As with Haflidson, Alanis was eager to explore her creativity no matter what the style of music was. Also like the sessions with Haflidson, Vanderburgh would play some prepared ideas on guitar or keyboards for Alanis. She would counter with melodies and lyrics. Together they would sketch out the rest. The collaboration produced a trio of songs: "Angel of Mercy," an aggressive "groove thing with a kinky edge to it"; the delicate, melodic "Believe Again"; and "Spectrum of Color," which Vanderburgh says was heading in the direction of "Hand in My Pocket."

All were ultimately recorded as demo tapes with little more than guitar accompaniment to Alanis's voice.

While many of the people Alanis linked up with were open and accepting, one collaborator says he was aware that Alanis's reputation within Toronto's music community was less than stellar. Her image as a teen dance act lingered and hindered her attempts to be taken seriously as an artist. When he told his friends who he had been working with, Alanis's name was greeted with sneers. The writer also recalls once taking Alanis over to a friend's house to rehearse a song with a drummer. A few members of a rock group were hanging around at the time, and while they were all attracted to her physically, behind her back they mocked her enthusiasm and spirit. In hipper-than-thou Toronto, her outlook was occasionally interpreted as naïve, insincere, or "spacey."

"She kind of had a showbizzy persona that could turn people off," the songwriter says. "I got a little tired of it, to be honest with you. She was kind of like an actress. Always: 'HI! HOW ARE YOU!' and that kind of thing. You weren't sure exactly where she was."

Despite the parade of collaborators, the results frustrated Alanis. She never really got exactly what she was after, someone willing to let her stretch out with her songwriting. Once, in mid-collaboration, she launched into her poetic, "stream-of-consciousness" style. When she stopped, her partner gave her a scolding look: "You can't do that. I don't think John Alexander or anyone at MCA would be very happy about this." On that occasion and many others, Alanis respectfully finished the song, walked out of the studio, and never gave the new song a second thought. "I'm not trying to paint myself as a martyr, but I don't think I was confident enough as a songwriter to say, mid-song: 'This is wrong! I am leaving!'" she says. "I think that would be a little disrespectful."

Consequently, there are now dozens of unreleased Alanis Morissette songs floating around the Canadian music business. The marquee value of her writing credit alone could land these songs on any record, but Alanis has resisted attempts to exploit her name and early work. Most of the people she worked with who wished to record the songs have asked her permission and accept her desire to leave the songs in the can, unreleased.

Although she worked seven days a week during her time in Toronto, Alanis grew so discouraged by her experiences with other musicians there that she seriously considered giving up on any hopes of finding a fruitful collaboration. "There was really no one I was connecting with in a cerebral, creative way at all. It became very disheartening." She and some of her would-be collaborators apparently had different agendas. Alanis was in search of an identity and was trying to find her artistic footing, while the hired-gun writers were in search of a lucrative hit. It's hardly surprising, then, that so many of her partnerships failed to flourish. Then a friend suggested Alanis work with songwriter Terry Sawchuk, who was at the time an engineer at Arnyard Studios in Toronto, where he worked with such artists as Wild T & The Spirit and the alternative band Our Lady Peace (which would later serve as opening act for the Canadian leg of Alanis's Can't Not tour).

Finally, Alanis clicked with someone. Their sessions together began in the fall of 1993, and they were "pretty laid back," according to Sawchuk, and quite different from what Alanis was used to. Trying out so many different styles with different writers can be an awkward process (Alanis compares it to blind dates), but Sawchuk's approach was much more relaxed. He credits his studio experience with giving him the ability to be creative on the fly. When artists arrive at the studio, their expectation, at $70 an hour, is that the engineer will be able to get creative "at the drop of a dime," no matter what their style or working method, he says. So Sawchuk had learned to be flexible and open to new ideas. And while some of the other writers were working to get a track on her album, that wasn't Sawchuk's motivation. "People were more interested in proving themselves, as opposed to trying to get more out of her," he says. "If the collaboration helped her out for her record, or if it was a song that was going to be on my record, that was great. But I can't say we had a goal in mind. It was just taking it from the song."

Moving between guitar, piano, and bass at that first session, Sawchuk worked up an instrumental track with Alanis, and got it down on his four-track tape machine. He could see Alanis attempting to write without the linear, traditional song structures that often held her back, and he had the good sense to stay out of her way as she ran with an idea.

The basics of their first song, which became known as "Comfort," were completed in two or three hours. Sawchuk describes it as "a kind of dark ballad, a very cold song," reminiscent of Cyndi Lauper's hit "Time After Time." They didn't spend time analyzing their method. It just evolved naturally. Once Alanis reached what Sawchuk calls her "comfort zone," the music flowed.

Altogether, they created about a half-dozen completed songs "and a ton of little sound bites and ideas." Some of them were solid. Some were promising starts. Some were dead ends, and some were just plain embarrassing. But in the creative process, artists need to let themselves write a bad song in order to discover the good stuff, Sawchuk says. That kind of anything-goes approach must have been a revelation to Alanis, compared to her previous experiences working on her two MCA albums, where several collaborators would compete to get their part included in the song.

Most of Alanis's songwriting partnerships were strictly professional, but her collaboration with Sawchuk grew into a lasting friendship. Eventually, songwriting became secondary in their relationship and Sawchuk and Alanis simply began to hang out together. She took great delight in socializing, something he believes stemmed from her career having occupied so much of her time during her teen years: "Having a major recording deal while you are in high school, I can't say there's a lot of time in there, with shooting videos and writing and recording, to meet a lot of people."

The pressures of her school days were now gone. And although she was living a modest lifestyle, the small income she received from MCA meant she wasn't out waiting tables to pay her rent. That left her plenty of time and energy for being creative and enjoying new experiences.

Meeting new people and having some encouraging songwriting results lifted her spirits.

Although she missed her family and stayed in touch with them, she enjoyed going out to see bands in Toronto and attending the odd record-release party. One night, she joined Sawchuk at the record launch for Our Lady Peace's album *Naveed*, and across the crowded room, she spotted a familiar face from Ottawa. It was Laury Schedler, her competitor from the Vocal Warz contest in Ottawa.

The two embraced and caught up on how they had each arrived in Toronto. Both were working on singing careers and neither knew a lot of people in the city. They soon discovered they had been living around the corner from each other for months without knowing.

They started hanging out after that night. Schedler found that Alanis still seemed to be searching for a direction, was "kind of broke," and needed some activity and companionship. Schedler was working at a fitness club, so she arranged a membership for her friend, and the two drove to the club together regularly, which gave Alanis a break from her nonstop songwriting.

Schedler still hoped to make her own record and found Alanis to be a source of insight and inspiration. She admired Alanis for having accomplished so much, so early in her life. "Take your time for your first album," Alanis advised her. "You don't have anyone breathing down your neck to get another album released. This is your first album, take as much time as you want and make it exactly what you want because you won't get another chance at a first album."

The two had a lot of fun going out to see bands, performing at the occasional songwriting showcase, and going to parties. Schedler got to know Alanis well: "She was a listener, rather than a talker . . . She didn't talk about herself a lot. She didn't like to brag about anything. And if you asked her how things were going, she'd say: 'Great! Amazing!' And I loved that."

One night Alanis called Schedler to see if she would go with her to a party that Kurt Swinghammer, a Toronto musician/artist Alanis was interested in, would be attending. "We have to go to this party. I have alanis

Onstage at the Ottawa Congress Centre in March 1996. It was Alanis's first home-town show since the success of *Jagged Little Pill*. Denis Cyr, Ottawa Sun

The cover of Alanis's second Canadian album, *Now Is the Time* (1992). MCA Music Publishing

November 1995, in concert at
Metropolis in Montreal, just as Alanis-mania
was gathering steam. A few years earlier, Alanis had snuck into the
same club after auditioning for *Star Search*. *Jeff Bassett*, Ottawa Sun

(Top) Onstage at the
Ottawa Congress Centre in
March 1996. *Denis Cyr*, Ottawa Sun
(Bottom) In concert at Metropolis in
Montreal, November 1995. *Jeff Bassett*, Ottawa Sun

During a rehearsal for the 1992 opening ceremonies for Winterlude, Ottawa's winter carnival, Alanis practises her number.
Jeff Bassett, Ottawa Sun

Posing in a Juno '92 sweatshirt, Alanis crosses her fingers for good luck just before heading off to the ceremonies in March 1992. The crossed fingers must have worked: she won most promising female vocalist.
Moe Doiron, Ottawa Sun ▶

Alanis poses backstage at the 1992 Juno Awards in Toronto with her statue for most promising female vocalist. *Mark O'Neill*

During a break from shooting *Music Works* in Ottawa, 1994, Alanis shares a laugh with Billy Cowsill (centre) and Jeffrey Hatcher from the group The Blue Shadows. *Derek Ruttan,* Ottawa Sun

A promotional poster for Alanis's show in Seoul, Korea.

Vancouver artist Bob Masse's striking poster for the Vancouver stop on the summer 1996 Can't Not tour.
Bob Masse, courtesy Bob Masse Studios

ALANIS MORISSETTE

FRENTE
OUR LADY PEACE

WEDNESDAY·JULY 31
GENERAL MOTORS PLACE

PRINTED IN CANADA

Onstage at Metropolis in Montreal, November 1995.
Jeff Bassett, Ottawa Sun ▼

something for Kurt," Alanis told Schedler. But after talking with him there, Alanis announced: "Okay, I'm over that now . . . I don't like him anymore," and they left.

Another evening, the pair had dinner with their neighbour Greg Torrington, a transplanted Ottawan who was now working in Toronto managing musicians. During the meal, Torrington slipped into his stereo a tape of a band he was considering signing called Sal's Birdland — the new project by Alanis's former producer Leslie Howe and friend Louise Reny. But Sal's Birdland was a million miles from the chipper pop of One To One: this sound was guitar-heavy, downbeat, and laced with Reny's sharp, occasionally profane wordplay. According to Torrington (who managed Sal's Birdland for a time and currently handles Schedler's career), Alanis loved the music and took particular delight in Reny's song "So Fucking Happy," saying: "This is amazing . . . I can't believe Reny's singing 'fuck.' Oh, that's so daring, so bold."

As much as she liked to spend time socializing, Alanis was strict about giving herself time alone. She and Schedler could hang together, but when it was time for Alanis to be by herself with her thoughts, she would take off. "She needs her own space," Schedler says. "She doesn't want to live with anybody. She likes to be alone and she needs that time."

Alanis also did not let her social life interfere with her commitment to find a new songwriting collaborator. Possibly her most significant songwriting union during her time in Toronto came entirely by accident. One day, she called Peer Music's David Baxter and interrupted a songwriting session he was holding with Tim Thorney, the veteran songwriter she had shared a table with at the 1992 Juno Awards. Thorney had always admired Alanis and was surprised to learn she was in Toronto, scrounging for collaborators. He called her and the two got to know each other over the phone.

Thorney had a solid track record as a singer, songwriter, and composer of music for commercials. Canadian singers Burton Cummings and Cassandra Vasik have covered his songs, and The Tractors and Garth Brooks have unreleased covers of his material.

Thorney seems like another unlikely collaborator for Alanis, but the chemistry was immediate. Alanis surprised him by arriving at his place in an old pair of overalls. The last time he had seen her was at the Junos, looking very different "in one of them winning-the-Juno-dresses," he chuckles. The face-to-face meeting picked up where their phone conversations had left off, with a lot of laughter and "keeping each other off balance."

Like Sawchuk, Thorney recognized that in order to unleash her full creativity, Alanis needed plenty of room and no restrictions. "She was just so perfect to write with. There were no rules. But I remember her sitting on the floor rhyming in stream-of-consciousness. Every time we tried to do something, she would say: 'Come over here, come over here.' It was like a dance or something, and we kind of went through it that way." They worked up a beautiful ballad called "Used to Run" — the first of several collaborations. "You could just tell she was riding some sort of wave. She was just perfect. Her melodic sense was perfect. Her lyrical sense was great."

Thorney and Alanis quickly became close friends. At one point, Thorney learned a friend of his in Nashville was dealing with cancer, and he convinced Alanis to drive down with him to "Music City." Thorney got to spend some time with his friend and he and Alanis explored the city. They weren't too impressed, and after some meetings with people at MCA (and possibly some attempts at songwriting by Alanis), they pushed deeper into the land of grits and blues and landed in Elvis's hometown, Memphis. The laid-back vibe of Memphis was much more to their liking.

As they drove back to Toronto, dressed in the same clothes they had been wearing for four days, and "smelling funny," Thorney asked Alanis what her shows would be like, once she released another record. "What are you going to dress like? What's the thing?" he asked.

"What do you mean?"

"What's the showbiz thing?" Thorney said. "What are you going to wear?"

"I'll wear this," Alanis said, referring to the clothes they'd been living in for days. Thorney laughed and shook his head: "Boy, it's going to be interesting."

Back in Toronto, they performed "Used to Run" at a songwriting showcase, and Thorney recruited her to provide some atmospheric vocal sounds on an album he produced for Canadian singer Tom Jackson — a non-verbal, skat-singing style she would later explore in greater depth on *Jagged Little Pill*. But like other collaborators, Thorney found some people in the Canadian record industry were ready to write Alanis off. "A lot of people thought she was over," says Thorney. "And I would say, 'Have you heard her sing? Is this not a real thing?' She's twenty and she can just do anything. She can sing quietly. She can sing in any key. Whatever key you write the song in, she can figure out a way to sing it."

Thorney may have been the older, more experienced partner, but he says he didn't teach Alanis anything about songwriting. All he had to offer was a non-judgmental attitude and an open, creative approach. "I think she found in me someone who is fairly optimistic. I can recognize truth in a song form. I never stopped her from doing anything. I never said: 'Maybe you should get back to this,' or 'This song is going away from a hit chorus.'"

Alanis and Thorney talked a lot about the process of songwriting and they came to the conclusion that the rational, self-conscious part of the imagination is what holds writers back from their best work. Their only rule was, "damn expectations and be fearless." Alanis didn't care what anyone thought and was willing to jump in and try anything. And Thorney didn't want to be the one "sitting on the shore saying the water is too cold." He jumped right in after her.

The results with Thorney were encouraging. Finally, here were songs that she felt good about, and that captured what she called her "stream-of-consciousness" songwriting method. Alanis describes her work with Thorney as a "magical experience" and even now she hopes to continue collaborating with him.

But she still believed she needed to find a different sound. Despite dozens of collaborations, she still didn't feel she had found a new direction for her music. The move to Toronto had been a valuable exercise in giving the young singer "life experiences." But it had proved largely fruitless at providing material for a new album.

"Her frustration was she had a lot more to say, but because she was still growing, she wasn't really a great musician yet," says her manager, Scott Welch, who kept on top of her progress in Toronto from his base in Los Angeles. "She was frustrated that she had a whole bunch of ideas but couldn't translate them yet."

If her chances of collaborating successfully in Canada seemed slim, so were her hopes of releasing a new record with a Canadian label. Because MCA distributed her Ghettovale albums with Leslie Howe, she still had connections there. A source at MCA confirms that a tape of some of Alanis's new songs did make limited rounds at the company. Obviously, the new material was a far cry from her previous, dance-oriented work, but, evidently, it also wasn't up to her full potential, a fact even Alanis now acknowledges. Although the singer herself was still popular at MCA, the label politely passed on any hope of succeeding with a third Alanis Morissette record.

In fact, before any album would come to fruition, she'd have a brief stint as a TV host.

11

Inside the
Music Works

She sat on a drum riser, with what can only be described as a determined smile frozen on her face. Somewhere, someone was counting backwards from five. A red light blinked on above a TV camera positioned a few feet from the singer's face.

"Hi! I'm Alanis. And this is *Music Works.*"

She was dressed in an amber chamois shirt over an untucked white tee, loose-fitting black pants, and chunky, shiny black boots. Behind the TV camera sat a silent, obedient Ottawa audience, recruited by the program's publicists to help stage *Music Works.* The show was a new venture for the Canadian Broadcasting Corporation and constituted a brave attempt at programming in two significant ways: first, it represented an increasingly rare foray into creating original programming in regional broadcast centres like Ottawa instead of at the CBC's head-quarters in Toronto; second, at a time when music videos were being provided nonstop by MuchMusic and MTV, *Music Works'* novel concept was to show musicians playing before a live TV audience, as though they were in a bar or nightclub.

"This studio will soon be filled with music from a Vancouver-based band whose sound is New Country rock," Alanis continued. The camera had framed her so the grafitti-covered walls in the background were tilted at odd angles, like the scenes inside Catwoman's lair on those old episodes of *Batman.* The studio itself was built inside a former CBC Ottawa truck garage. A stepladder, crates, road signs, and layers of graffiti cluttered the set, meticulously transforming the garage into something akin to a recklessly assembled, grubby rehearsal hall. Or, to be more specific, a rehearsal hall filled with choking clouds of mechanically generated, light-enhancing theatrical mist.

"These four dynamic guys have a sound that is both refreshing and familiar."

The floor director signalled for applause. The audience responded and somewhere, a disembodied voice yelled "Cut!" Headset-sporting technicians scrambled on set to make lighting and camera adjustments. Alanis walked over to the makeup artist for a few adjustments of her own. The heat from a humid summer night, combined with an array of hot studio lights and heavy atmosphere from the smoke, made for an occasionally uncomfortable working environment. But as usual, she was to all outward appearances ebullient.

"All right! You guys sound great. You're working up here," she said after two songs by her guests The Blue Shadows, on this final night's taping, and jokingly mopped the brow of the band's guitarist Jeffrey Hatcher.

She turned to the quartet's forty-five-year-old singer, Billy Cowsill, whose craggy features prompted one writer to describe him as looking like something Rolling Stones' guitarist Keith Richards would wear on his knuckle. About twenty-six years earlier, Cowsill had been a member, along with his mother Barbara and his younger siblings, of The

Cowsills, America's "first family of music," and the group sold millions of sunny pop records, like the 1967 smash "The Rain, the Park and Other Things." During a stint in Vegas, Cowsill grew restless and quit to embark on an odyssey of high and low living that took him to Oklahoma, Texas, and the Northwest Territories, before settling in Vancouver and eventually linking up with Hatcher to form The Blue Shadows.

"So," Alanis said, turning her telegenic gaze on Cowsill, "I understand you've been doing this for a long time."

Cowsill chuckled and shook his head, and the hostess immediately recognized the unintentional suggestion: oops, that makes you sound like Granddaddy Rock.

"I mean that as far as experience onstage," she stumbled to recover from the unintended slight. "Great band," she said of The Cowsills, although their heyday predated her birth by about seven years. "And from what I understand, The Cowsills inspired The Partridge Family," she added, referring to suggestions that the fictional pop ensemble was loosely based on The Cowsills' career. He muttered in the affirmative, adding that his life was apparently the basis for seventies teen heartthrob David Cassidy's character Keith.

"Oh darling," she gushed. "I'm not worthy!"

For all the talk-show breeziness of the interview, in hindsight, one can't help but wonder if Alanis didn't notice the parallels between herself and Cowsill. Both were adolescent stars who enjoyed a brief, early flash of fame. Both were trying to forge a new identity with newer, more substantial music. Both were having trouble being reconsidered by the music business, which seemed determined to freeze them in that limited, early, frivolous role. The main difference between them was that Alanis had only been at the task of reestablishing herself for a matter of months. Cowsill had been at it for more than two decades.

"It's been great chatting with you guys. You guys are great and good luck. It's been a pleasure listening," she purred, before turning to her audience, both in the studio and out there in TV land. "Thanks for joining us. And have a really great night." Cue applause. Roll credits.

Music Works was the brainchild of CBC producer Adele Cardamone, who conceived the program while talking to high school students about a proposed youth program.

"As I was interviewing teens, all they knew was American bands. Guns N' Roses, Pearl Jam, Bon Jovi," she says. "I said I want to do something for Canadian music. It's not going to be the big headliners like Bryan Adams and Celine Dion. We don't have the bucks to pay them, and they don't need the exposure."

If the show was to succeed, it needed a host to introduce the acts and to be the thread that would draw the audience back each week. As a TV producer, Cardamone had worked with Alanis a couple of other times over the years on telethons and other TV specials. She kept Alanis in the back of her mind for whatever opportunities TV could offer — as a performer or even as an on-camera host. She immediately thought of Alanis for *Music Works*.

"I didn't want your average host, your unknown. I wanted somebody to be a little more knowledgeable about the music business. I wanted someone from a musician's point of view. Alanis was quite good that way. She would address questions that perhaps your MuchMusic VJ wouldn't do," says Cardamone. "She has a great look. The camera loves her. She has a great charm and warmth. I liked the fact that she was from Ottawa. I knew I wanted this to be a young adult show, and if the show was going to continue, I wanted somebody who could identify with the young adult audience."

When Cardamone brought the then unnamed show to the station, the CBC liked the idea of Alanis as host. And they hoped that the new show would not only work as a showcase for up-and-coming Canadian bands, but would also be an ongoing showcase for Alanis herself. "No one really developed her in the Ottawa area. They used her on telethons, singing the national anthem here and there. But really, no one took her and developed her. We were hoping to do that with the show, before things got great for her."

Cardamone called Georgia Morissette with the offer, and she passed along her daughter's phone number in Toronto. Alanis said yes immediately. And she must have been eager for the chance. She didn't hesitate to commit to the program, even though shooting was months away, in the spring and early summer of 1994, and at that point, there was a very real chance the program would never survive the labyrinthine development process and make it on air.

Even though she was just getting by on a small stipend from her publisher, Alanis's eagerness to be a part of the new show could not have been financially motivated. The *Music Works* money was not great, and by agreeing to do the show so early, Alanis tied up her schedule for eight months. The lure was the show itself — talking to musicians and being taken seriously as a part of the music business. With sponsorship from a shampoo company, Cardamone finally had a green light to begin shooting at the muggy height of an Ottawa summer.

Some sponsors approached for the show had felt Alanis wasn't a big enough name to host. Others had confused her with Alannah Myles, another Canadian singer whose celebrity had already crested at the time. But it's a measure of how far Alanis's stock had fallen in the Canadian music business that the only serious opposition to her taking on the hosting duties on the new show came from within the record industry, including some of her fellow musicians. Some of the acts approached to appear on *Music Works* — particularly some of the hard rock acts — actually refused to do the show because Alanis was the host. Cardamone says there were some label representatives who also expressed doubts about Alanis. "A lot of them questioned whether she knew much about alternative rock music, which is kind of a joke now, when you see what she has done."

In fact, Alanis proved to be well-informed about the business, and even came up with the name for the series. Cardamone had toyed with "Jammin' in the Warehouse," but Alanis offered up "Music Works," commenting that when musicians compose, they'll often agree on an idea by saying "that works." Her suggestion may also have been influenced by her experience at the similarly named Songworks workshop in Toronto.

When it came time to promote the show, a few critics politely lauded Alanis's job as TV host, although a writer in Hamilton commented that "the cheesy fawning and coddling of the show's lightweight host Alanis is a bit much to take." In Toronto, the epicentre of the Canadian music business, *Music Works* was ignored. The *Ottawa Sun* was the only paper interested in interviewing Alanis about it.

"I've watched a lot of interviews where everything comes across very stiff and formal," she told the paper's Rick Overall. "I've also been in a situation where a lot of my own personal interviews have been very black-and-white, where no one felt relaxed and neither party felt like we'd accomplished much. I wanted to create a situation where each one of these artists could say a few things to the public that might not ordinarily get explained. Whether it be how they write, how they met, or how they interact within a group format."

Whatever the misgivings of some of the proposed guests and sponsors and the disinterest of some critics, Cardamone said she had no regrets about hiring Alanis for the job. She was attentive, professional, low-key, eager to learn, and easy to work with. "I've worked with hosts who count the lines and count the minutes they are on the air. None of that with Alanis. She is very mature . . . When she made comments they were very intelligent, never naïve. She was knowledgeable about the business. Not just music, but television. She respected my role, the cameraman's role, audio's role."

During the taping of that final episode, Alanis had her eye on a member of The Blue Shadows, but it wasn't Cowsill. Before the show, as the group was in the makeup room, she walked up behind bassist Barry Muir, who was then thirty-six, and offered him a neck massage. When Muir left the backstage area, she followed him and the two struck up a conversation. A member of the show's staff was later dispatched to convey a message to Muir: "Alanis really likes you."

While the band was packing up its gear and heading to the hotel, she stopped by to say her final good-byes, then approached Muir. "I really like you, and I'd like to see you." Muir said he was too tired to go out, so she offered to drop by his hotel.

Muir — who was in the process of splitting with his wife at the time — sat up alone in his room until midnight, laughing at himself for thinking the young, pretty singer would actually follow through on the tryst, and drifted off to sleep.

At 2 a.m., his phone rang. Alanis was down in the lobby and wanted to come up for a visit. As she made her way to his room, Muir freshened up by sticking his head under the tap, wetting his hair. When she spotted his dripping locks, she commented on how odd that was, to be showering at two in the morning.

"I think it's kind of weird for you to show up at my room at two in the morning," he replied.

Muir says the pair stayed in his room, "watching MuchMusic and smooching," until dawn. He told Alanis about his early career — playing as a teen in a wedding band in Saskatoon, heading as a naïve seventeen-year-old to Vancouver with the dream of making it in the Canadian music business, and lucking into a job with eighties Canadian hitmakers The Payolas (a favourite of Alanis's) and Barney Bentall's Legendary Hearts, before recording his own unreleased solo album and joining The Blue Shadows.

Alanis, in turn, told him about her plans to find a new direction for her career, and her relationship with Dave Coulier. "I never saw *Full House*, but when she said her boyfriend acted on it, I thought she meant the young, good-looking guy with the dark hair (John Stamos). She said: 'No, the other guy, the blond guy.' I thought: 'That's kind of unusual.'"

Muir and his band left town the next morning, but over the course of the next year, he and Alanis kept in contact. She called him a few weeks later, and was surprised when Muir's (soon-to-be-ex) wife answered the phone. The bassist hastily explained his marital situation, and Alanis was disappointed by the news. Soon, however, Muir was single, and he and Alanis maintained their long-distance relationship, although Muir says it was platonic.

Whenever his group was performing in Toronto, he always made sure to link up with her for coffee. He believes Alanis was interested in developing a romance, but Muir says he was uncomfortable with the difference in their ages, and demurred. He was happy to have her as a friend, though. "We hugged and kissed, and she expressed her feelings for me . . . I thought she was too young. But she's a beautiful woman," he says. They talked of how Alanis had never really fit in with girls her own age, how she had lost contact with many of her friends and was now meeting a new set of musician friends.

Muir once sent her a CD by American singer Sam Phillips as a gift, and she said the music was a great inspiration for the new material she was working on. He also sent her a picture of himself, which Alanis carried with her, and he still has the postcards she sent him. During their talks together, she described her plans to experiment with new writers and new styles of music, and even her hopes of writing with Muir. Despite her efforts to involve him in her career, Muir says he never gave it serious consideration.

"I never took her seriously," he admits. "I just thought of that mall singer, Debbie Gibson–type thing."

But Alanis sounded dead serious about becoming a singer and song-writer of substance. And although Alanis has described that Toronto period as bleak, Muir says his lingering impression of her is upbeat. When he confessed he had momentary doubts about his future in the music business, she chastised him and asserted how lucky they were to make music for a living.

"I always picked up an incredibly strong, positive vibe. Relentless . . . I got the impression she was really happy with being a musician, with the people she knew in the industry, and felt very fortunate," he says. "You could tell she was in a learning pattern. She wanted to change her image, that was for sure. She didn't want to be the clean-cut girl from Ottawa. She wanted to make an attempt at doing something a bit grungier and more organic, something that would make people notice the change. I always thought: 'What do you mean? Acoustic instruments?' I never knew what she meant, but I sure heard it on *Jagged Little Pill*. An honest, personal record. It sounds exactly like she described it at the time."

But to get there, Alanis decided she would have to expand on the process of learning and writing she began in Toronto. And she would have to do it somewhere new.

At Scott Welch's suggestion, Alanis had started making trips to Los Angeles to try writing with people there, too. There had been talk of her returning to Ottawa for a second season of *Music Works* and if she had, the plan was for her to perform some of the new, unrecorded material she had been working on. Had she opted to stay in Canada, Alanis may very well have unveiled her new look and sound to a Canadian TV audience. Instead, fresh from the challenge of adjusting to life in Toronto, she decided to take on an even greater challenge and move to L.A.

12

California

A lanis lay face-down on the hot Los Angeles pavement and did as the men with the gun said. As her two assailants rummaged through her meagre belongings, one single thought raced through her mind: Don't take my lyrics.

She had only been in L.A. a short time. She arrived in the summer of 1994 to stay at a friend's place in Beachwood Canyon, hoping to expand the writing and learning process she had begun in Toronto. She was coming back from a work-out session and was stopping off at home for a quick shower before heading off to a studio for some songwriting. As she pulled the car into the back of her friend's place, the two thieves made their move. Alanis had no concern about losing her money or documents. All she cared about was her book of song lyrics. And after the men escaped, she was relieved to find they hadn't touched it. "I would have taken a bullet for that one," she says of the lyric book, some of the songs in which would evolve into material for her next record.

"Welcome to L.A.," said the police woman dispatched to investigate her robbery.

For someone reared in the gun-phobic environment of Canada, the incident should have had her booking the red-eye back to Toronto. Add to that the fact that Alanis had already experienced the unique terror of earthquake aftershocks shortly after her arrival. But far from discouraging her, the incidents seemed to fire her determination. Exposure to dangerous situations was a necessary wakeup call that forced her to realize that she wasn't invincible. "I was just tired of being naïve, or what I felt was naïve," she says. When she had told her friends in Toronto about her decision to relocate south, they were surprised by her boldness. Even artists with record deals and solid financial and personal support are often reluctant to make the jump to the United States. "She was not afraid to swoop down to L.A., all that stuff. A lot of people up here in Canada have deals, and they would just not have the balls to do something like that, to go where the action is," said her Toronto collaborator Steve Haflidson.

Scott Welch described the decision to move to Los Angeles as a "shotgun approach": write with as many people as possible, and they'd know when she matched up with the right person. Just like in Toronto, Alanis lived on some money from MCA Publishing and Welch. Not much, but enough to get by while she established herself. After staying with friends, and flying back and forth between Los Angeles, Toronto, and Ottawa, she eventually settled in, renting a two-bedroom place in Santa Monica.

Apart from big-city crime and shifting tectonic plates, the City of Angels provided a whole new set of stresses and experiences for the young singer. "I think some of that came from the fact that there was a bigger cultural difference between Los Angeles and Canada than I thought there would be," she says. In a city where entertainment people thrive on big talk about their work, Alanis says her "quiet confidence was misconstrued for passivity." To keep up, she trained herself to speak out and be "a bit more overt."

When Alanis left for the coast, Laury Schedler gave her the number of her friend Brian Bowie, a filmmaker originally from Ottawa. Alanis called him several times, without luck — he was in the process of preparing to direct his own feature film, *Pennies from Hell,* and kept putting Alanis off. Bowie, who worked for years in Chicago, says he is part of a large group of pals — several are comedians — who hang out together. He finally agreed to bring her to a party and introduced Alanis to his circle, which quickly became her Los Angeles family.

"I have known this group of friends for years and years," he says. "We all hang out together. Alanis melded in very well." Like so many others, Bowie learned that Alanis possessed a wisdom well beyond her years, and also like others, describes her as "an old soul." When she and Bowie were out in groups, Alanis's "quiet confidence" made her come across as a bit of a wallflower. But when they'd speak on the phone, she would relish the chance to explore philosophical topics and ponder the meaning of life.

"When she talks to you on the phone, she is really able to converse . . . She gets very deep very quick."

Alanis even invited Bowie and his gang to her Santa Monica pad. She had set up one bedroom as a studio for music and painting (a new artistic outlet she had begun exploring), and the house was filled with candles. Bowie recalls that at her party, the place was illuminated entirely by candlelight.

Although she had a new circle of friends and a new round of collaborations, Alanis still hadn't found her footing as a songwriter, but there was progress and growth. Welch started receiving calls from her new songwriting partners, letting him know that despite the underwhelming results of their collaborations they could see Alanis possessed immense talent that was just waiting to break out. When he met her for lunch, Alanis played Welch a tape of fifteen new songs. Ten of those showed signs of greatness.

"Man, you are on the right track," Welch told Alanis after listening to the tape. "Just stay with it."

Despite all the setbacks and disappointments, Alanis knew the partner who would help her reach her potential was out there somewhere. "I had faith. I had nothing that had proven that faith right yet, but I knew it could be. No matter where, when, and who and what situation." After many false starts and disappointments, Alanis finally joined forces with a songwriter who, in Welch's words, "pried open the door."

▽

In the fall of 1994, Alanis showed up at Glen Ballard's home recording studio in suburban L.A., and within fifteen minutes, they were finishing up their first song. Alanis knew her search for the right collaborator had ended.

Ballard had already enjoyed an amazing career. Originally a keyboardist, he landed a job as a staff producer for Quincy Jones, and along the way, he worked with a string of remarkable talent in just about every style of music, including Aretha Franklin, Natalie Cole, Chaka Khan, George Benson, Barbra Streisand, the Pointer Sisters, Paula Abdul, Al Jarreau, Earth Wind & Fire, George Straight, and K. T. Oslin. He also wrote and arranged Michael Jackson's anthemic "Man in the Mirror" and worked with the platinum pop-vocal trio Wilson Phillips. In all, Ballard has produced or written records that have sold nearly 100 million copies. MCA Publishing, which handles Ballard's catalogue, hoped his Midas touch would work with Alanis.

"I walked into the studio and the spirit was so warm, so positive," Alanis recalls. "They put us together, thinking that we'd probably come up with some more pop dance stuff. But when Glen and I got together, we knew immediately that this was something that was very special."

That first song they teamed up on that day was called "The Bottom Line," and they composed eight or nine more tracks during that session and a second get-together a few weeks later. Publishing records also list "Closer than You Might Believe," "Keep the Radio On," "No Avalon," and "Why Can't I" as early Ballard/Morissette works, and to this day, Alanis describes some of them as her favourites.

They took a break over Christmas, but she and Ballard were committed to making a record together. Finally, her goal of writing more personal music seemed within reach.

But while she may have at last been on the right track for her career, Alanis still wasn't completely happy in her personal life. The pressures of relocating to L.A., dealing with the frustrations of her early career, and always hiding her anxieties under a mask of tranquillity mounted and threatened to derail her. Suddenly, just as she seemed to be getting her life together, it all started to come undone.

13

Sanctuary

On a flight home in December 1994, Alanis was rushing to complete her last-minute Christmas cards when a strange feeling swept over her. Without warning, she became overwhelmed by intense feelings of anxiety. She tried to hold herself together, but found herself convulsing with sobs.

After the flight she began suffering fainting spells. It was like her previous breakdown at her parents' home, but much more intense. This wasn't a tailspin that a pep talk from Mom and Dad could pull her out of, but something more serious.

The crying and fainting didn't stop. She was terrified and later sought the advice of a doctor. Was it a physiological problem? Was it psychological? It was as if a reservoir of repressed, untended-to emotions suddenly breached its banks. The anxiety and uncertainty, the repressed feelings and frustrations that Alanis the Pop Princess had never been able to express in her personal life or her music were suddenly demanding attention.

"The universe was telling me that if I didn't stop and be still and start thinking about it and releasing it, it was going to subtly remind me. Or not so subtly remind me," she says. She learned that the inundations of fear she experienced are known as anxiety attacks — a sensation not uncommon among people in their mid-twenties, but something she had never before encountered to this extreme. "I became quite familiar with them thereafter," she says grimly.

Resolving those issues meant recognizing the division between the internal and external world. She had to discover that what happened on the outside — people's judgments and expectations and reactions — were beyond her control. She could only command what happened to her "internal world."

By learning to focus on her inner self and to accept and resign herself to the external circumstances, she came to a happier, healthier place. "I know I can't control the external world, which is the reception to what I create," she says. "There's an internal world, which is my personal development and creative development and spiritual development. That's the only thing I can control. I can control how much knowledge I feed myself, but I can't control what happens around me with people's perceptions of it."

To some, it may seem like a trite discovery. But for someone who grew up onstage coping with people's judgments and maintaining a façade of self-assurance, all the while feeling unable to deal with the inevitable anxiety and insecurity, it must have come as a revelation. "I thought fame and the public persona would make me peaceful. And it wasn't very conducive to a peaceful lifestyle. So I learned how to write for my own reasons and write for myself."

By abandoning external approval as a goal, Alanis was able to heal herself. As frightening as the entire episode must have been, it was a crucial phase in reaching her next artistic plateau. When she got back to writing music with Ballard after the Christmas break, it would not be a denial of those demons. They would be the subject of her music.

"The world has a way of not putting up on a pedestal those that are pure and vulnerable and maybe naïve, insecure," she says. "They throw adulation in the direction of someone who is charismatic and intriguing and cocky and self-assured. Society made me believe that if you are being vulnerable and expressive in that area, you'd get shot down and taken advantage of." Expressing vulnerability in her art would not only make her a happier person, it would also lead to the most satisfying and accepted music of her career.

When she reunited with Ballard in February, it was obvious something had changed. The music they had already made together was great, but clearly, Alanis needed to write about the emotional ordeal she had been through in the past two months, and, in a sense, for most of her life. They set aside those early songs and started again with renewed energy and intensity. Alanis wanted to go off in an entirely new direction, and Ballard was happy to follow her, wherever her instincts would take them.

"It wasn't a cakewalk," says Ballard. "We were really ruthless with the stuff. Really, we would toss out three or four ideas a day, which we should probably go dig up, because they are good. But these new songs were better."

They knew they were on their way.

▽

Why was the collaboration between Ballard and Alanis so successful? Welch believes that Ballard was the first collaborator who didn't try to dictate creative terms to Alanis. As well, he is a skilled musician and producer and was able to translate her ideas into songs. "For some reason, they are soul mates," says Welch. "He was able to translate this wealth she had in her head, and able to help her to communicate it."

One look through his resumé and it's apparent that Ballard's work has been skewed towards pop and smooth soul balladeers. Perhaps his collaboration with Alanis was fuelled by the fact that both writers had something to prove. Both had been typecast as generators of slick pop, and both wanted to get to something deeper.

At the start of their collaboration, Ballard made no conscious decision to step out of character and go against preconceptions about his work, but he found that he relished the opportunity to eliminate people's expectations. And as for Alanis, she was in a new country where her past work was unknown, and she had finally found a partner eager to entertain her every stylistic whim. "We both started with a clean slate. It was like a sanctuary for us. We were finally in this environment where we could do whatever the hell we wanted to do," she says.

They knew little of each other's work, as well, which meant they had no expectations of each other. As Ballard comments, "It was almost like we could leave all the baggage outside the door and approach it like we were just going to please ourselves." Working without preconditions gave them an invigorating freedom. Songwriting became a shared adventure.

Their working method was simple. She would sit on the floor. Ballard would perch in a chair. They'd both take acoustic guitars (an instrument Alanis had been learning) and fool around with melodies and lyrical ideas and see what happened. When they really got rolling, Alanis would fall into a kind of trance-like state. Sometimes, minutes after writing the song, she would have no memory of its creation. "We would just open ourselves to it," she says. "Sometimes within five minutes, sometimes within two hours, it would just start and it would all come out and the song would be done. A lot of times I would listen to these songs and never even remember writing them. I just remember driving back to the studio to write another song the next day, listening to this song we wrote the night before, and I couldn't believe it. I couldn't remember it."

Because they were working in Ballard's studio anyway, they started recording the songs as they were being written. *Jagged Little Pill* is actually the sound of two writers in the full flight of collaboration. A rough version of the music and a one- or two-take vocal were recorded within minutes of completing the songs. The instrumental details were filled in later by session players. Alanis added ragged touches of harmonica to several tracks, another instrument she was dabbling with.

"In 95 percent of what you hear on the record, the ink is not dry on the page. It is the most extraordinary thing I've ever seen," Ballard says. "The more time we got to spend together, the deeper the connection for me, of understanding intellectually and emotionally where she was coming from. Really it was more a matter of her getting deeper into what she wanted to say, and feeling the freedom to do it, finding an outlet for it."

The turning point was a song called "Perfect" — one of *Jagged Little Pill*'s most effective tracks. "It was probably one of the most overwhelming spiritual moments that I've ever had," Alanis says. They were in the middle of writing another song when they abruptly stopped and launched off in a new direction. Twenty minutes later the entire song was done. Alanis went into a vocal booth and recorded the vocals heard on the final record in one or two takes.

With its exhortations to keep smiling, move faster, go farther, and don't screw up, "Perfect" has been widely interpreted as an attack on parental expectations. But that seems unlikely, considering Alanis's declaration of her parents' unconditional support. More likely, the hectoring voice in "Perfect" is the internal voice that pushed the teenaged Alanis relentlessly towards perfection. Finally, with Ballard's help, she was able to articulate those long unstated fears and weaknesses and purge them in song. "A lot of it came out because I had been repressing it for so long," she says.

For Ballard, this was a strange new creative experience that helped him in his own collaborations with other artists. He began to see that he hadn't been using all of the artistic judgment he could. "Alanis certainly empowered me to be an artist with her, to say, 'Do your thing.' We weren't trying to write for the market, so it was extremely liberating for me to have my creativity unleashed . . . I hadn't felt there was a situation for me to pour a lot of my music into."

Alanis has frequently compared the power of her connection to

Ballard to a kind of religious awakening. "It was like God's way of saying to me, 'You've been working your ass off, and I'm going to give this to you. Enjoy it, please,'" she told *Details* magazine. She was so pleased about the way things were going with Ballard, she phoned songwriter Terry Sawchuk back in Toronto and played him six of the new songs.

Sawchuk was astounded, and nearly dropped the phone in disbelief. Although his collaboration with Alanis had been positive, he could tell that now she had finally said what she had always wanted to say with her music. All her hit-and-miss experiences with other writers had finally paid off.

When Alanis made a return trip to Toronto shortly after she started working with Ballard, Sawchuk asked her to demonstrate the technique the pair had used. They poured cups of coffee, sat down together at Sawchuk's piano, and Alanis outlined their "stream-of-consciousness" writing style. By the time she was through demonstrating, the pair came up with the basics for a track called "Superstar Wonderful Weirdos," which Ballard and Alanis later finished and recorded, but cut from the final track listing. (Ballard and Alanis also recorded a version of "Used to Run," her collaboration with Thorney, but it, too, was dropped from the album's track listing.)

Alanis also called her former collaborator Leslie Howe and played him demos over the phone. Even over the long-distance line, the work impressed him. Especially the lyrics, which he says stack up against anyone currently writing in popular music. "It is a different style," he says, "but I am totally proud of her in her lyric writing."

But while Alanis let her old collaborators in on what was developing in the studio with Glen Ballard, her new L.A. friends had no idea. Brian Bowie repeatedly asked her for a taste of the music, but she insisted she didn't want any of her friends to hear her new songs in advance. Finally, Alanis let him hear a sneak preview of the work.

"What do you think?" she asked Bowie.

He paused for a full minute before replying. "You know what, hon? Get ready for one hell of an adventure."

The bulk of the record was completed in a matter of weeks, a

▲
Alanis breaks up while struggling with her luggage the morning after her 1992 Juno win. *Jeff Bassett,* Ottawa Sun

◄
Cuts like a NYF. Alanis poses with the members of New York Fries, her brief, early attempt at rock 'n' roll. *Poster courtesy Richie Wright*

At a December 1991 press conference to promote Winterlude, Alanis shows off a button. She would become a frequent feature of Ottawa's seasonal festivals. *Jeff Bassett*, Ottawa Sun

I love Winterlude 92 J'aime

Alanis, arm-in-arm with friend, singer Louise Reny. *Courtesy Louise Reny*

Surrounded by her friends, Alanis parties with John Alexander (far left) and Frank Levin at the Blue Cactus Bar in the Byward Market, Ottawa. *Courtesy Frank Levin*

With Senators official Randy Burgess at a news conference to announce Draft Express, a train hauling hockey fans to Montreal for the draft. *Moe Doiron, Ottawa Sun*

Andres de Castillo lends support on guitar as Alanis performs for hockey fans on board the Senators Draft Express to Montreal, June 1992. Ottawa Sun

▶ Alanis looks shaky as she rehearses singing on skates for Winterlude ceremonies in January 1992. *Jeff Bassett,* Ottawa Sun

Important friends: (from left), Mila Mulroney, Stephan Klovan, Alanis, and John Alexander, during a gala charity event at the World Exchange Plaza in Ottawa, *circa* 1992. *Courtesy Stephan Klovan* ▼

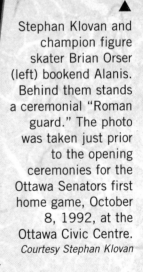

Stephan Klovan and champion figure skater Brian Orser (left) bookend Alanis. Behind them stands a ceremonial "Roman guard." The photo was taken just prior to the opening ceremonies for the Ottawa Senators first home game, October 8, 1992, at the Ottawa Civic Centre. *Courtesy Stephan Klovan*

◀ Alanis and a "Roman chariot" driver help herald the arrival of the Ottawa Senators in October 1992, at a celebrity horse race event at the Rideau-Carleton Raceway. *Jeff Ducharme*, Ottawa Sun

▲
Alanis clowns
with staff and
crew from the CBC
show *Music Works*
(from left, Carolyn
Schjerming, Adele
Cardamone,
Michelle Muntean),
at CBC studios in
Ottawa, summer
1994. *Dino
Cardamone, courtesy
Adele Cardamone*

▶
Alanis visits
Lindsay Morgan
during recording
sessions in Bright,
Ontario, in 1994.
Courtesy Lindsay Morgan

▲
In concert at the Ottawa Congress Centre in March 1996. *Denis Cyr*, Ottawa Sun

◄
Leslie Howe, who masterminded Alanis's two Canadian albums. *Jeff Bassett*, Ottawa Sun

Alanis shows her true patriot love on Parliament Hill, June 29, 1993, most likely during preparations for Canada Day Celebrations on July 1.
Jason Kryk, Ottawa Sun

phenomenal achievement, considering many artists spend months or years chasing the desired sounds. Because of the speed and quality of their output, Ballard suggested to Welch that he hold off on searching for a record deal and let them finish the album at his state-of-the-art home studio. "I'm working on something really special here, I just feel it," he told Welch. "I just want to work on this, I don't want to do anything else. We can make the record here. I believe in this so much, I don't want to stop to worry about a record company. Let's just not stop."

Ballard was concerned that inviting a label into the creative process could dilute the purity of their vision. If the album was submitted before it was finished, he worried that there would be plenty of unsolicited record company advisers happy to dictate how they should complete the project. "It was important from an artistic standpoint to keep control and not get a bunch of opinions until we were satisfied ourselves." Welch agreed to let them finish what they'd started, before shopping for a label.

During the recording, Ballard gave special attention to Alanis's vocals, pushing them up to the front of the mix, giving them an almost conversational, confessional quality. Technically, that effect was achieved by recording her voice with a 1954 AKG C-12 microphone. For whatever unfathomable, technical reason, Ballard believes that that particular piece of equipment — which he no longer loans out to anyone — is perfect for Alanis's voice. He also sent her voice through vintage tube limiters and preamps, "so there is a lot between her and what's going to tape. Not a lot, but the right stuff." But mostly, the vocals work "because she is such a great singer. I tried not to mess with it. I tried to get it as pure as possible on tape . . . Mostly it has to do with what is coming out of her mouth."

"Your House," an a cappella track hidden at the end of the album, started out with an instrumental backing track, but they decided to let Alanis's voice carry the song. Without even a beat or melody to guide her, Alanis sings the fanciful tale of a woman who snoops around her lover's home, listens to his Joni Mitchell albums, and then stumbles upon evidence of betrayal. "It is not even synched up to the track.

She's not singing to a click track. It modulates up and down, up and down. And she was nailing it," says Ballard.

The song would later become a frequent set-closer when she hit the road, and Alanis told *Spin* magazine that the lyrics came from her experience of staying at the Hollywood home of a man she had a crush on. Many details, including her new interest in Joni Mitchell, were true. The snooping and betrayal were inventions. "That is the only song on the record that's not one hundred percent true . . . I get burned at the end of the song because if I had really snooped around as much as I wanted to, it would have been wrong," she told *Spin.*

If the Christmastime breakdown had been like a reservoir of pent-up emotions breaking open, now Alanis seemed to be able to control the floodgates herself and direct the rush of feelings into her music. On "You Learn," she reconciles with her uncertainty and confusion and draws strength from setbacks. "Forgiven" explores her relationship with the Catholic church and includes a reference to naughtily jumping into a fountain — perhaps an oblique reference to her Paris video adventure. The comforting "Hand in My Pocket," which was captured in about forty minutes, articulates her feelings of displacement and alienation when she left Canada, and she suggests it came directly from the emotional meltdown she experienced after the move to L.A. "There is always a part of me that is still very introverted," she says in explaining the song's repeated image of keeping "one hand in my pocket."

"In many ways, as time went on, I became somewhat of a recluse. When I was not in the studio, I lost the incentive to just go out there and put out all the time, because I would work so hard in the studio. There would be a knot in my stomach as the weekend would approach because I knew I would have to go out to the city again and work on my personal life. So there is always a part of me holding in, and me staying close to me. And there was another part of me that was working hard and reaching out."

And the song "Head over Feet" contains an obvious parallel relationship to that of her alliance with Ballard, whom she now describes as "my best friend." "He provided an environment for me to just write what I wanted to write," she says. "And a lot of what I wrote about came out of philosophical discussions he and I would have for an hour or two during lunch, before we wrote. He was not only capable of understanding my own thoughts, but he would accept it and pull it out of me. Musically we are on the same wavelength."

The important point, says Ballard, is that their commercial achievements with *Jagged Little Pill* were built on constructing a very personal statement and conceived without consideration of the marketplace. "She is very grateful and appreciative that she has connected with so many people, so quickly. But she is also mindful of the fact that what got her here is being herself . . . We weren't trying to please anybody . . . We were trying to communicate with each other, first. And then, when we were successful doing that, it seemed to work for everyone else."

Of all the songs she and Ballard created, the most emotionally demanding was "Mary Jane." Her old family friend Jacqui Morgan says Alanis has told her the song was written about their friendship. (When Alanis performed an early showcase concert in Vancouver, Morgan watched tearfully from the edge of the stage and presented the singer with a rose at the song's conclusion.)

Once they were well on their way towards completing the album, Welch began to accompany Alanis to meetings with several labels. The two would bring in rough tapes of the songs to play, with Alanis fielding questions from the record execs. The process of shopping for a deal typically gives both artist and label a chance to feel each other out. Will the singer give the label lots of input into the completion of the album? Will the label give the artist enough freedom to make the kind of record he or she wants? Often, it's a process of compromise and the artist's work is blunted in the name of marketability before the public even gets to hear a note. It was exactly that kind of whittling away of rough edges that Ballard, Welch, and Alanis hoped to avoid by going to the labels once they could hear her music fully formed. If they liked it, fine. But compromise would not be a part of the negotiations. They would have to take Alanis and her songs as they were.

Meeting with the labels gave Alanis her first taste of the insidious sexism that exists in the record business. In the past, working with Lindsay Morgan or Leslie Howe, she never had to confront the condescending and crass attitudes that linger in the executive suites of some major labels. Being young, and being a woman, she encountered what she describes as "the old school mentality": "Their respect for art is very low on their priority list. Their very sort of money-hungry corporate way of thinking did not mesh at all with my purist, artistic outlook."

After some of the meetings, Alanis's frustration would be so obvious, Welch would shake his head and give her a hug, to let her know he understood and was there to support her. Alanis now says, "I was just putting up with so much. I walk this fine line constantly of having respect and being diplomatic with people and then just standing up for myself. Where do you draw the line?"

The encounters provided fodder for one of her most livid songs, "Right Through You." In Canada, the song has been interpreted as a broadside at a record industry that embraced and then rejected her, but Alanis makes it clear the song was "not about the last ten years, it was particularly about the last ten months" leading up to the release of *Jagged Little Pill.*

The song's final verse sees Alanis as "Miss Thing," a wealthy star revisiting the same label hotshots, taunting them and flaunting the fact that she left their names off her album credits. The song has been widely quoted as evidence of her self-assurance, that she predicted her own fame. But she insists the verse was written in jest. At the time, she was living such a low-rent lifestyle, the very idea of revisiting her detractors as a "zillionaire" was a pie-in-the-sky revenge fantasy — not a prediction. She had no idea how the public would react to her new work. She just knew it was the music she had always hoped one day to make.

14

The Deal

During a brief break from final sessions for her album, Welch and Alanis had a meeting with yet another label boss to talk up the idea of signing Alanis. But just as discussions were getting started, Alanis surprised her manager.

"We worked on something last night," she told Welch and the record exec at the meeting. "I want you to hear it."

Alanis played the tape of her newest composition. It began with a shuffle drum beat and an intimate whisper before erupting into a volley with uncompromising declarations of anger and pain. The lyrics were brutally honest and sexually graphic, seething with righteous indignation; and the music propelled them beautifully. The song was "You Oughta Know."

The label exec didn't get it and wasn't interested in Alanis or her music. But it didn't matter to Welch. He recognized that "You Oughta Know" was a landmark. "When I came out of the meeting, I was doing cartwheels. It was just such a breakthrough for her as a songwriter, to start out with. On top of that, it was a song that was going to make people react. That's all you can ever hope for," says Welch.

Surprisingly, such a tempestuous song started as a calm, rational telephone conversation with a former lover. But what Alanis couldn't bring herself to say to him found its way into the controversial lyrics, which bait the unidentified ex-lover about his new relationship with an older woman.

"I was probably more mad at myself for being in that position," she recalls. "For close to a year, I didn't admit how I felt about it. And then I got off the phone with him one day and I was completely freaked out. I just wrote down everything I felt for the first time. I'm a very rational, conscious person a lot of times, especially when it comes to people's feelings. I would never hurt someone on purpose, so I would never say that to him. But I got off the phone, and I thought: 'I owe it to myself to be completely honest about how I feel.'" So she unburdened herself, filling up three sheets of paper with her resentment and fears. Those lines were later fashioned into lyrical form and combined with Ballard's musical contribution.

Whether consciously or not, the structure of the finished song paralleled the very symptoms of repression and release that Alanis was working through in her private life. It starts off quiet and conciliatory with subtle instrumentation and polite words that suggest buried emotions and a congenial outlook. Then the track erupts with all those unstated feelings of betrayal and anger. The images accumulate and the stakes rise with each verse. In a way, "You Oughta Know," mirrors Alanis's own discovery of the power that can come from dealing with pain, instead of burying it under a placid disguise. And despite the challenge of continually stirring up those difficult emotions on record and on stage, once she tapped into this new style of songwriting, there was no turning back. "When I was writing it, I don't think

I took into account that I'd have to perform it night after night. And every time I sing it, it's like I'm communicating it again for the first time. And I know, when I do more than one or two shows a week, I am spent . . . There have been a few nights where I sort of go over the edge a bit. I try and hold it in, for the sake of finishing the show. But the alternative is to write songs that aren't that personal. And it would be easy to do interviews and easy to perform. I think that would be a crime."

That record exec who passed on the promise of "You Oughta Know" may not have understood the song's power, but five major labels were definitely interested. Welch had waited until the album was "90 percent done" before he started seeking a corporate home for Alanis. Waiting enabled the manager to be more selective. He even ranked the level of interest among the labels, with ten being the most eager to sign Alanis. One of the labels rated a ten out of ten. The label chief was desperate to sign her, but Welch felt this wasn't the right home for Alanis. Two other labels rated eight out of ten, and a further two labels rated a lukewarm six out of ten.

Welch doesn't name the interested labels, but sources indicate that Atlantic was one of the imprints making serious overtures. Maverick, a label set up especially for Alanis's childhood favourite, Madonna, as part of her contract with Warner, earned an eight in Welch's ratings.

As it turned out, the lawyer who was representing Alanis joined in on the action. One of his partner's clients was Guy Oseary, the twenty-two-year-old A&R rep at Maverick. Alanis's lawyer asked his partner to get Oseary onside, and so when his colleague met Oseary on an unrelated matter, he played him the tape, and, according to Welch, Oseary "flipped." Maverick's interest heated up, but Oseary said the label would not commit until they saw Alanis perform live.

Usually record labels see an artist play live before they do any signing. Welch says that Maverick was nervous since Alanis's performing experience was limited: "O Canada" at hockey games; singing along to pre-recorded dance tunes while opening for Vanilla Ice or at charity events; some New York Fries bar gigs; a couple of low-key turns at songwriting showcases in Toronto. If she failed to impress the Maverick execs with her live work, it could have been a deal-breaker.

Welch set up a mini-concert in Ballard's studio for a small group of label executives. Oseary, Maverick general manager Abbey Konowitch, and president Freddy DeMann attended. With the executives seated a few feet away, Ballard played acoustic guitar and Alanis sang. Then Ballard set up backing tapes of some of the songs from the record and Alanis sang the vocals live. If she was nervous, she didn't show it. "That's enough. Let's go outside," the Maverick crew interrupted. Welch stepped out into the studio hallway. They hammered out a deal on the spot. Now all that remained was for Alanis to decide whether or not to sign.

The relationship between record labels and artists, particularly for a musician with a strong vision, can be rocky. Personal expression doesn't always jibe with sound financial practice, and Alanis says the decision to sign with any label was not an easy one: "That the whole corporate world and the art world can work together is pretty amazing. I like to think I found the happy meeting of the two at Maverick. But we'll see," she says. "Before I met Maverick, I had kind of resigned myself to sign with the lesser of all evils. There was no company that understood me and was willing to sort of ensure the longevity of it."

Alanis knew that, unlike her previous label experience, her new record could not involve hiding behind any artificial image or sleek marketing campaign. "There were a million things that were very confusing when it came to having to decide. It could have been one of the biggest decisions I would have to make over the next couple of years. To make it under that extreme amount of pressure . . . It was extremely difficult."

She wrote out a list of all the labels that had expressed an interest in her work and wrote out the pros and cons associated with each. "The cons would always outweigh the pros and I would wonder what I was going to do. Then I met Maverick."

Ultimately, the deal hinged on Maverick's willingness to embrace Alanis as she was, rather than try to fabricate an image. She liked the fact that they were attracted to an artist with a sense of her own identity, that they were secure enough to take on a singer who knew what she wanted.

Prior to signing, Alanis told friends she was unsure about signing with Maverick and reluctant to meet with Madonna, who is nominally the head of Maverick. She actually leaves most of the day-to-day operations to her staff, but she does have a say in whatever projects the label gets involved with. Naturally, she wanted to meet the new singer her label was hoping to sign, but Alanis feared the sheer force of Madonna's personality would overwhelm her judgment about which label to choose. When the two eventually met, they got along famously, laughing the whole time.

"I love Alanis's record," Madonna later told *Spin* magazine. "I know I'm supposed to say that because she's on my label, but I just thank God for people like that. I'm really sick of the other music that's just so full of: 'The world sucks, everything sucks, or just no hope.' That bores me."

The deal negotiated with Maverick ended up being fantastic for Alanis. Welch assumed the album would sell a few hundred thousand copies, more than she ever sold during the Canadian phase of her career, but little more than a good starting point for an American artist. He was hoping for 250,000 to 300,000 so Alanis could "get her feet wet, people would at least know her name."

Because of that, Welch says, a standard label deal, which would include an advance payment against future royalties, would have left her without much money coming in. Instead of taking money up front, Welch and Alanis's lawyer negotiated a higher royalty percentage per record. (Now that the record is over twenty-times platinum, she stands to make even more money.)

But before Alanis was free and clear to sign with Maverick, there was still the issue of her 1988 deal with Ghettovale. That deal was for up to five albums, and Alanis had only ever recorded two with Leslie Howe's company. Although lawyer Heather Perkins-McVey had advised Alanis to have the deal set aside once she turned eighteen, that was apparently never done. The contract was still valid when Alanis went to California.

It's not uncommon for new artists to sign deals early in their careers with managers or labels or producers, only to move on to bigger and better projects, and then have the old alliances come back to haunt their newly lucrative careers. Obviously, with so much water under the bridge and so much at stake in her new career in California, there was no chance Alanis would be willing to work with Ghettovale on a third album. Nonetheless, Howe's company held the option on three more albums.

How the issue was negotiated and resolved has been a subject of much speculation. Alanis now confirms that Howe agreed to set aside the Ghettovale deal and clear the way for Maverick in return for a percentage of revenue from *Jagged Little Pill*. "We drew up a whole parting-of-the-ways agreement. And that's all I can really say," says Alanis.

The resolution — seemingly negotiated on the presumption that *Jagged Little Pill* would sell a few hundred thousand copies — would have seemed at first like a quick and inexpensive way to unburden Alanis from the Ghettovale pact. In the wake of the record's unprecedented and unexpected success, though, any percentage of *Jagged Little Pill* could be worth millions of dollars. Which would mean, hypothetically, that Ghettovale, which had risked $100,000 and the future of Distortion Studios on Alanis's career, could in return receive a massive financial windfall. Alanis declines to say how much money was involved in the transaction, and Howe won't even confirm there was any kind of settlement involving revenue from *Jagged Little Pill*. "If there is a settlement agreement, obviously I am getting money from this and I just don't want people knowing my financial affairs," he says.

Alanis's own comments on financial matters have been confusing. Some of her friends suggest she was unhappy about her past business dealings. One friend said Alanis had a "bad taste" in her mouth about the whole era. Alanis told *Spin* magazine: "There are certain mistakes that you make when you're 16 because you're ignorant . . . Let's just say that I'm still paying for the mistakes I've made. I think of it as my tuition for The College of Music Career."

Welch comments that "what she's feeling, I think, is she made some mistakes not taking care of her business." But, he points out, whatever setbacks she may have encountered earlier in her career have given her insight and prepared her for this point in her career. Now she's able to make the right decisions, because of her hard-won experience.

Alanis now had a record and a record label. But she still needed a title for her album, one that would encompass the whole experience. She settled on *Jagged Little Pill*, a line from the record's most conciliatory track, "You Learn."

"The line right after it says it feels so good swimming in your stomach. And that just implies that whole era, when I was immersed in growing up. I didn't realize there were lessons in it. And only in retrospect can you realize why it was all happening," Alanis explains.

Once the record was done, all the labour and anguish and uncertainty faded, she adds. "I don't have any painful memories of working on it. I just have emotional ones."

▽

As *Jagged Little Pill* was being prepared for release, Alanis took a quick trip home to Ottawa, and one night, while out at a bar in Hull, she spotted Richie Wright, her drummer from the New York Fries days.

She sounded him out on the idea of moving to L.A. and playing in her band. Wright, who had no strong ties to home and was free to pick up and move, readily agreed. She also spoke to her friend, bassist Barry Muir, about working on *Jagged Little Pill* and invited him down to rehearsals for her band, as well. But his band was about to head into the studio, and Alanis didn't press him on the invitation. (In fact, neither musician ended up playing with Alanis's band. Wright now plays with a band called US, which covers "You Oughta Know" in its bar set. Muir still plays around Vancouver with three-quarters of The Blue Shadows, under the name The Sugar Beats.)

Back in L.A., Alanis took to the nightclubs, checking out bands with her friend Brian Bowie. They went to the Las Palmas theatre to see some bands that were so dreadful, Alanis apologized to Bowie all the way home. But they did meet Dave Navarro, formerly guitarist with Jane's Addiction and currently of the Red Hot Chili Peppers. Bowie remembers Navarro, who had heard the still-unreleased album, describing Alanis's music as "absolutely amazing." Producer Jimmy Boyelle recruited Navarro and Chili Peppers bassist, Flea, to play on his remix of "You Oughta Know," which had been pegged as the first single from *Jagged Little Pill.* Navarro also suggested that Alanis hire Jesse Tobias, the guitarist he was replacing in the Peppers' lineup.

Because of the army of freelance players in Los Angeles, Alanis hired a special consultant to seek out likely candidates, and they hosted two full days of rehearsals, with Alanis singing with three different players every half hour.

She finally narrowed down the candidates and decided on drummer Taylor Hawkins, guitarist Nick Lashley, and bassist Chris Chaney, along with guitarist Jesse Tobias. Hawkins and Lashley had both played with Canadian singer Sass Jordan. San Francisco native Chaney comes from a jazz background and, according to *Musician* magazine, tried out as bassist with Seal's band before getting the call from Alanis. The lineup was complete.

"Those guys stood out," Alanis told *Guitar Player* magazine. "I was auditioning not only their musicianship, but also if they understood what I was singing in my songs. I mean, I never came out and posed the question, 'Do you understand where I'm coming from?' But I did get a sense from them as to whether they did. It's a very precious thing to me, the creation of art. So I wanted to get a sense that they were excited by it, too."

More important than pure musicianship was the fact that each player nicely balanced experience with an enthusiastic, unjaded outlook. Touring was going to be a new experience for Alanis, and she needed to be surrounded by people who would see it as an adventure, not as another year on the concert tour grind.

To celebrate the completion of the album and the formation of her band, Alanis hosted a party for about one hundred people at Ballard's studio in April 1995. Brian Bowie and some of her L.A. friends were there, as were Madonna and senior people from Maverick.

With her characteristic flair for creating atmosphere, Alanis had the entire room illuminated with candles, which cast a warm glow over the crowded room. As the guests looked on in anticipation, Alanis and her new band premiered the songs from *Jagged Little Pill*. No one there that night could have guessed what would happen once that album was unleashed on the public.

15

Head over Feet

Timothy White tore open the seal on yet another courier package of cassettes and fished around inside for the contents. As editor of the music industry bible, *Billboard* magazine, White received dozens of tapes each week from record companies eager to enlist the magazine's support in creating a buzz about a new record. He had been a writer and editor for *Rolling Stone* and *Spin,* and author of the respected Bob Marley biography *Catch a Fire* and an exhaustive survey of the Beach Boys and California culture called *The Nearest Faraway Place.* White was one of the most respected names in popular music criticism, and he had been hired six years earlier to revamp *Billboard.* Despite its status as one of the most important music publications, he thought that the magazine had become overwhelmed by music industry news, with very little musical content. His job was to put the music back into *Billboard*, and he took it very seriously.

After emptying the contents of the package onto his desk, he found three tapes from Warner (the record label that distributes Maverick). The cassettes bore only the name of the artist, the album, and song titles. No press kit. No hype. Over the course of an average work day, the editor often sampled as many as thirty preview cassettes. White dropped the cassette marked "Alanis Morissette: Jagged Little Pill" into his office tape deck and pressed play. What he heard stopped him cold.

"The guiding instinct is to always find something that doesn't sound like anything else. This really fit that bill," White says. He was so taken with the tape, he played it over and over. At one point, the magazine's talent editor, Melinda Newman, stuck her head in White's office and said, "Man, you are really on a jag with this record."

White replied: "Have you listened to this thing? It dropped from the moon. It is so one-of-a-kind."

Part of White's job was to write an editor's column. He resisted the idea, and instead decided to use it as an opportunity to practise a "dense, old-fashioned" style of rock criticism; that column, "Music to My Ears," has been White's pulpit from which to hold forth on any subject that strikes his fancy. In recent years, White has shown a particular interest in the Canadian music scene. He had backpacked across the country during his high school and college years and initiated special annual issues of *Billboard* devoted to the Canadian scene. "Canada, to me, seems like a foreign country. It doesn't seem like an extension of anything else. I just relate to it as a foreign country and I enjoy it enormously," White says.

In the late eighties, White noticed that Canadian artists had moved away from their traditional aping of American and British styles and started to produce something a little more original and more emblematic of the Canadian experience. More importantly, Canadian audiences had embraced the new music and started buying it in impressive quantities. "I predicted somewhere in 1990 that Canada was going to be like what England was a few decades before. I just thought Canada was going to become a really important place."

And so, for that particular May 13, 1995, issue — still ahead of the official release date of *Jagged Little Pill* — White opted to tell his readers about an unheralded young Canadian woman and her new album. "Morissette's often severe writing voice has the crackling certitude of someone who's long past tentative vulnerability or impulsive confessionalism," White wrote in an interview and analysis piece headlined, "Morissette's Jagged Self-Healing."

"Because she dares to stand naked in her remembrances, the narrator allows herself no comfort zone for self-righteousness, and as she builds steam in her incantatory checklist of public indignities and private indiscretions, the singer's wounded outrage mingles with a gathering courage that gives the listener a giddy desire to cheer her on." White went on to predict that *Jagged Little Pill* "is likely to fascinate listeners on both sides of the border."

In the meantime, Maverick's Abbey Konowitch took a preview copy of selected songs from the CD to an informal meeting with Lisa Worden, music director at KROQ, the influential, top-rated alternative radio station in the Los Angeles area. Konowitch gave Worden the expected lecture on how strongly the label believed in the project, and how they had great expectations for *Jagged Little Pill*. And then he played "You Oughta Know."

"We didn't really know what to think of it," says Worden, who thanked Konowitch and agreed to consider the song at an upcoming "music meeting" — which was held by staff to decide what records make it on air at the station. About forty records were played, discussed, accepted, or rejected at that meeting. But Worden says once she heard it again at the meeting, the power of the song hit home. There was no doubt about the future of "You Oughta Know" at KROQ. On May 16, 1995, just days after the meeting with Konowitch, and still weeks before the album was even due to be shipped to stores, the radio station became the first to play "You Oughta Know," unwittingly unleashing the commercial juggernaut that *Jagged Little Pill* would become.

"It hit us like a brick in the head," says Worden. "And we just knew what we had. We put it on the air right then and there. And it got phones from the first time we played it." ("Getting phones" is radio-industry parlance for audience reaction to a given song. A record that generates lots of calls from listeners means it gets "phones." And a song that generates lots of phones, in radio-land, is a good thing.) As far as KROQ was concerned, "You Oughta Know" was a great thing.

"You Oughta Know" was more mainstream than many of the records that attain number one phones status at KROQ. Usually, the title is won by hard-hitting songs that have some controversial element — the musical equivalent of a screaming tabloid headline. Shock rockers Marilyn Manson are more typical. But with its risqué subject matter, "You Oughta Know" qualified. "We know what kinds of records we put on will receive phones," Worden explains. "And we knew 'You Oughta Know' would be a phone record. But this record was the number one song the week after we put it on. It was just huge."

KROQ's support of the song — one station in one city — triggered a rush among radio stations. Suddenly everyone had to have it, and the label hadn't even started its formal campaign for airplay. The record hadn't even been shipped to radio as a single when KROQ started playing it.

Billboard's Timothy White says a Warner executive told him the excitement generated by the record caught the company off-guard. "You Oughta Know" was snowballing before the star-making machine could give it a push. "We're literally trying to figure out a way to get out in front of it," the exec told White.

The song allowed Alanis to quickly break through and connect with millions of listeners, but much of the attention focused on decoding the identity of her mystery lover. A few select lines have been, in Alanis's words, "dragged through the scrutiny mud," as various names were brought forward. Her old collaborator Leslie Howe was so disturbed by gossip about his relationship with the singer, he called the *Ottawa Sun* to clear the air: "I don't want to be defensive or bitter. I want to be positively explaining what some other people and publications' misconceptions have been," Howe said. "And I don't want to be a hanger-on. We worked together, and we're friends . . . People are trying to pick a name and pin it on somebody. But I don't know what else I can say to say it was not me. Alanis and I were friends and worked together professionally. But we certainly never dated."

In fact, Howe was just one of several names that were bandied about as the unnamed lover who was the object of the song's ire. The U.S.-based tabloid TV show *American Journal* offered up the following suspects: *Friends* star Matt Leblanc, who appeared in a second video for her song "Walk Away" back in 1991 and was a brief but casual acquaintance; Senators' tough guy Mike Peluso, who told the TV show he never had an intimate relationship with Alanis, but added, "One percent of me says maybe it is (about me), and 99 percent is not" (when told of Peluso's remarks, Alanis laughs out loud); and Dave Coulier, who friends say was her only serious romantic relationship.

Beyond stating that the lyrics were inspired by what she couldn't bring herself to say to her former boyfriend, Alanis herself has never publicly stated who the song was directed at. Nor has she indicated whether every element of the song was related to a specific relationship or whether she created elements of the scenario. She does acknowledge that Dave Coulier's name comes up most often in connection with "You Oughta Know." "I'm not going to deny or say yes to that, because I think it is wrong. I sort of laugh at it. That was the most public relationship, and it is a predictable answer . . . The truth is I am never going to tell who it was about."

Unfortunately, because of the public's infatuation with trying to identify the object of Alanis's scorn, the real motivation for writing the song has been lost. "When you are hurt, your immediate emotion is to protect yourself and get really angry," she says. "But in my estimation, anger is a cowardly extension of pain. I was in so much pain, the best way for me to release it at that moment — and it seriously was a snapshot one afternoon — was to be angry. And then a week or six months later, I wasn't angry anymore. But all of a sudden, the song is still angry. And people presume I am still, too."

It is perhaps understandable that the object of such an attention-grabbing song would become the object of speculation. But revealing the identity would play right into perceptions of Alanis the Avenger. In fact, Alanis says she feels love for the person whom the song is about and gratitude that he did break off the relationship. Declaring his identity would be cruel. "And if it was written for the sake of revenge, Lord knows, I would be plastering his picture everywhere. And I would never do that, because I have respect for him."

Despite her intentions, much of the attention the record has received is based on the perception that Alanis was a vengeful, angry woman — a perception skewed by the selection of "You Oughta Know" as the first single. There's anger on *Jagged Little Pill*, but the balance of the record was conciliatory and reflective. If "You Learn" or "Hand in My Pocket" or "Ironic" had been the first single, it's hard to imagine Alanis being typecast as the First Lady of Rage.

Scott Welch believes there is something in particular about "You Oughta Know," though, that energized her success. "That song came on the air, and millions of women went: 'That's exactly how I feel. That is IT! I want to hear that song again.'" And it's not just women. Welch points out that men have also been taken with the song: "There are some mental images there that are sexually driven; for men, it is a little bit of voyeurism. I think that drives it a little bit, too." As Timothy White says, "It is a woman's record that any open-minded man can enjoy. Any man who has ever fallen in love with a woman because he enjoys her poise and intelligence will like that record."

Alanis says she doesn't like to ponder why "You Oughta Know" connected with so many people, but she has her theories. "It excited people to see someone being that embarrassingly honest. And it validated their seemingly embarrassing emotions. Society does not revere people who admit they were broken-hearted and horrified in that way. When it is poetic and pretty, it is fine to express it. When it is harsh like that experience was, society wants to move away from that. So it may have been refreshing to those that felt how horrified they were by their breakups. They heard it and went: 'Wow . . . She's not embarrassed, so maybe I shouldn't be.'"

Her record did not represent the first time a woman had detailed her sense of betrayal in stark, often graphic terms. Marianne Faithfull's "Broken English" and P. J. Harvey's "Rid of Me" both cover similar territory, although neither enjoyed the widespread commercial acceptance of "You Oughta Know." Alanis suspects she benefited from society's long-delayed acceptance of "genderless" expression from women: "If Steven Tyler can say he's living it up while he's going down (from Aerosmith's "Love in an Elevator"), then why can't a woman say it, whether it is me or not?"

KROQ played "You Oughta Know" for months. In its highest rotation, it would repeat six or seven times a day. And when people got sick of that, they just moved on to one of the record's other tracks. "We definitely burned that song out. And we have gone on since to play about six other songs," Worden says.

Listeners may have tired of hearing a particular Alanis song after radio overplay, but they couldn't get enough of her. What happened at KROQ happened across North America, and then in almost every market that tracks record sales and airplay. Many who knew Alanis or heard the songs that would become *Jagged Little Pill* were convinced of their artistic merit. But no one could have foreseen a response that would be so immediate and so widespread. Most observers agree there just weren't any other strong-voiced, reasonably commercial-sounding young women on the radio at that time. And by unimaginatively signing and promoting a slew of new, young female singers in the wake of Alanis's success, the major labels have indicated they agree that Maverick had tapped into a previously underexploited niche of the market.

The number of tracks radio was prepared to play — in some markets, six or more songs were thrown into rotation — also helped drive sales. Record buyers are naturally more likely to purchase a CD with lots of familiar material, and the fact that *Jagged Little Pill* contained so many songs that could fit into so many radio formats helped cement its success. "She appeals to every demo. Women, men, young, old. So the album is great," says Worden.

To complement radio's embrace of "You Oughta Know," Alanis and her band drove around the desert for three days, and shot a video for the song at locations in Death Valley and, for the performance sequence, amid stone ruins they found in Nevada. Like the restraint-release structure of the song, the video for "You Oughta Know" works as a parable for Alanis's recent artistic and personal awakening. Intercut with fuzzy footage of the group playing in a bombed-out building are shots of the singer tromping grimly through a desert, lugging a suitcase. She opens the bag, pulls on some new clothes, and, by the end of the song, emerges from the desert into a flowered meadow. Alanis, after struggling through her own creative desert and hauling her emotional baggage, changes and moves on, happier and wiser, to a more rewarding place in her life.

Like radio, MTV in the United States and MuchMusic in Canada put the video for "You Oughta Know" into heavy rotation. And each of the subsequent videos followed suit — the curiously comforting rain-on-my-parade metaphor of "Hand in My Pocket," the creative-but-simple quadruple-Alanis road movie of "Ironic," the surrealist pastiche of "You Learn" (and its in-concert sequel), and the close-up, blithe gigglefest, "Head over Feet."

In fact, "Head over Feet" was shot after the record company had indicated there would be no further singles. Radio stations, led once again by KROQ, were still hot for another Alanis track, and started playing "Head over Feet" on their own initiative. The video was shot in response to the insatiable hunger for the CD.

White's original *Billboard* column was distributed with some review copies of *Jagged Little Pill*, and that doubtlessly helped set the tone for the generally positive newspaper and magazine reviews the record received. But White says he may have also played a part in getting Alanis Morissette simultaneous coverage in the two most widely read music periodicals — *Spin* and *Rolling Stone*. At a party in Manhattan, White, *Spin* publisher Bob Guccione Jr., and *Spin* executive editor Craig Marks were talking music when White brought up Alanis. "Man, you gotta put her on the cover. You gotta trust me, this is all I do for a living. I don't know rocket science, but I know what is going to be a giant hit," White told the pair.

Guccione outlined the magazine's publishing schedule, and White made a bold prediction based on sales forecasts and radio reports he had been hearing. "If you put her on the cover for this particular week, I can tell you, she will be number one the week the magazine comes out." So *Spin* gave Alanis her first cover story, and that week, White's prediction came true. The record hit the top of the charts. In a rare move, twelve days after *Spin* hit the racks with Alanis on the cover, *Rolling Stone* caught up by making their own feature on her into a cover story. The two magazines compete fiercely and rarely (if ever) feature the same artist simultaneously.

"*Spin* was a cover story and we agreed to that because they were the first people to get behind us," says Welch. "And at the same time, there was a feature going in *Rolling Stone*. And when the record exploded, they went: 'Hey! We're putting her on the cover.'"

Suddenly, it seemed like Alanis was everywhere — radio, TV, magazines. "It was all very fun and very exciting and very deserved," White says. "Nobody asked me to do that." In fact, as opposed to the typical record company method of gaining exposure — buying lots of ads, strong-arming blanket coverage, and generally firing up the promotion machine — all the support seemed to stem simply from people's enthusiasm. In the months that followed the album's release, two perceptions built up around Alanis's career: She was the beneficiary of a huge, expensive push from her record company, and she has attempted to divert attention from her history in Canada. Both are lies, says White.

No one hyped the record or prodded White to take notice of *Jagged Little Pill*. His decision to profile her in *Billboard* was purely a reaction to what he heard on the tape. "No one tugged my coattails. No one literally ever phoned." Because the tape arrived without a press bio or even any photos, it was Alanis herself who detailed, in a telephone interview with White, her past recording career in Canada. She volunteered descriptions of her early records, gave an account of her emotional ups and downs, and hid nothing. "She took great pains to explain every blessed thing to me," says White. "The fact that she concealed her background is such a bag of trash. She told me everything."

As to the rumours of expensive hype, if anything, the demand for access to Alanis far outstripped what she and Welch were prepared to supply. "I have turned down stuff most of the time you would die to get. We had no control over the fact that she got on both covers of *Spin* and *Rolling Stone*," says Welch.

Bolstering the early exposure, Alanis and her band appeared on *Saturday Night Live*, *The Late Show with David Letterman*, and the MTV awards, where they delivered a galvanizing performance of "You Oughta Know." In front of a star-studded industry crowd at Radio City Music Hall, Alanis and her band raged through the song with frightening intensity. Welch spotted everyone from Michael Jackson to Tom Petty leaping to their feet to applaud. "That audience was in shock. They were stunned when they finished," Welch says.

During a lull in the first round of promoting *Jagged Little Pill*, Alanis confided to Welch that when she was growing up, the ultimate dream for an aspiring musician was to appear on *Saturday Night Live* and land on the cover of *Rolling Stone*. She was alarmed by the realization that these things had happened so quickly, in the first six months.

Handling so much success, so soon, could be a tall order. Many young careers have drifted dangerously, even fatally, off-course because of the demands and temptations of fame. But by most accounts, Alanis was well prepared when success came her way. She may not have had much to show for it, but her earlier, modest taste of fame had readied her for the success of *Jagged Little Pill*. In a sense, she had been preparing for this moment her whole life.

16

On the Road

Alanis squinted into the semi-darkness of the tiny Ottawa nightclub Zaphod Beeblebrox and shyly addressed her audience. "You can come a little closer. I don't bite heads off."

But most of the 125 people in the club opted to keep their distance. Was it shock at the fiery performer — dressed in her new stage armour of leather pants and oversized silk shirt — who now stood in place of the perky pop princess the city had grown to love and then taken for granted? Or was it the sheer, frightening force of the five musicians onstage ploughing into the songs from *Jagged Little Pill*?

Although the group had only been together for weeks, they had already coalesced into a solid unit, creating cleverly — often radically — rearranged versions of the new songs. And now, here among the people who thought they knew her best, on the Byward Market bar strip where she used to sneak into clubs underage, the reaction was muted. But for anyone who really listened, there was no doubt Alanis had undergone a thorough artistic rebirth, and whatever the speculations about the sincerity of her new songs, there was no questioning her delivery of the material in person. "This is a song about someone I spent a lot of time with who frustrated me because he was selfish," she said by way of introducing "Wake Up."

What followed was a rendition of the song that was so fierce, it appeared to leave her shaken and on the verge of tears. Often after these early shows, Welch made sure no one came backstage for a few minutes to give Alanis time to compose herself, and from the start, her band members respected the potent and highly personal nature of the music and watched out for her.

But performing the material wasn't simply a matter of dragging her back over old, rough emotional ground. The shows also had a cathartic effect and gave her a sense of release. "I would be lying if I said I was up there being tortured every night," Alanis says. "There's a part of it that is good for me. If I continued to hold everything in, I would probably explode. And I would probably start losing it on people."

With his background in live concert sound engineering, Welch knew the value of touring — not just for Alanis but for the whole band. He hoped that sending them out to play endless tour dates would develop a chemistry between the players that would serve them well down the road. After the incredible success on the radio, his biggest concern was trying to hold it together with a band: "A band is like a football or basketball team. You have to work together to gel. You can do all that crap in a rehearsal studio, but you gotta play in front of people. My biggest concern was playing enough small places and keep it so she could have a chance to grow," he says. That meant travelling in a cramped van, performing in sweaty clubs, and staying in lower-grade hotels. It was time to hit the road.

Having Alanis and the band perform in small places like Zaphod Beeblebrox in selected cities would introduce radio and critics to her music and let the band find its legs as a touring unit before playing to large, paying audiences.

Whereas in the United States, no one knew of her previously, in Canada, where memories of her early days lingered, Warner Music had to be a bit more strategic in how they reintroduced Alanis. The band performed a thirty-five-minute set at the label's corporate meeting in picturesque, mountainous Banff, Alberta, to give the people promoting her new music in Canada the chance to "see she is real," says Welch. Then the tapes were played for critics, occasionally without identifying the singer, "just so the music would get a fair shake," Welch says.

The club tour was arranged before *Jagged Little Pill* took off, so that by the time she arrived in many of the cities, demand for tickets far exceeded supply. At a time when she could have been at medium-sized theatres, she was playing hole-in-the-wall bars. The temptation to upgrade the tour and grab bigger money must have been great, but Welch stuck with his original plan out of concern for the small-scale promoters who had taken a chance on booking the shows before the album became a hit. Many of the promoters were young and just start-ing out in the business, and pulling the dates could have caused severe financial hardship.

As a result of Welch's determination to keep the band in clubland, Alanis ended up passing on an opportunity to replace 1995 Lollapalooza dropout Sinead O'Connor. For an upstart act, it was perceived by some as a snub. But Welch says all the advertising for the shows and all the Lollapalooza ticket sales were finished, so they had already missed out on the festival's promotional benefits — performing in broad daylight before a rowdy festival crowd was pressure Alanis and her band didn't need just as they were finding their touring legs.

The whole road experiment worked because of the people involved, Welch says. "She's got a great group of people working with her, great spirited people. They hang out together. She has done a great job of being a musician with them and being the boss," says Welch.

In time, each of the players would come to establish their own pres-ence. Nick Lashley, who became Alanis's guitar tutor, supplied the atmospheric, heavily treated guitar effects. Jesse Tobias's aggressive guitar style bolstered the rhythmic power of the music. Bassist Chris Chaney was reserved and cool, while drummer Taylor Hawkins became a flamboyant fan favourite, and over the course of many months of touring, his lightning fills would play off Alanis's vocal flourishes with a kind of telepathic precision.

Touring so tirelessly for more than a year and a half not only helped the band find its stage legs, but it also forged a bond with her audience. Welch stood at the soundboard at these concerts and watched fans at the back of the hall sing along — not just with well-aired singles, but with every track on the record. He understood the importance of forging that link with her fans. If Alanis bonded with her audience, it would help her down the road because they would keep coming back to her music. "She is going to want to write what is in her soul and not what is going to get played on radio. And if you have built your fan base, they will go buy your record based on what you say. You won't be a slave to whether you have a hit on radio."

The pace was gruelling, and there were reports of the singer suffering from exhaustion. Welch denies that she was ever hospitalized because of fatigue. "She's young. She doesn't drink. She doesn't smoke cigarettes. She eats really well. And she doesn't do drugs. She takes care of herself," he says. But there was a need to balance her duties as a performer with the other demands on her time. They opted to cut back on interviews and focus on putting on as strong a live show as possible.

Alanis says the tedium of performing the same songs night after night was tempered by the sense that each audience had a different "personality" and presented a new opportunity to convey her feelings. "The only thing that I can liken it to," she says, "is if you wrote on a piece of paper something that you really, really believed in. And then I was to tell you that you were going to meet a new person every day and tell them your belief. While you may be reading the same thing every day, you are looking at a different person who is very open to hearing what you are about to say."

By the end of 1995, they had graduated to larger concert halls. In

November, she played Montreal's Metropolis club — the same dance hall she and Stephan Klovan had snuck off to after auditioning for *Star Search* so many years before. In the middle of an opening set by The Rentals, Alanis and her band mischievously crashed the stage with food purloined from the backstage smorgasbord and wrapped the players in paper towels as they played.

During her rapturously received performance of "You Oughta Know," drummer Taylor Hawkins performed an extended version of his shuffle intro while the singer paused to take a pull from a water bottle. The crowd spontaneously sang the whole first verse themselves. Alanis set down the bottle, walked to the edge of the stage, and asked: "Why are you so angry?"

The gesture, which would become a recurring element for much of the tour, was her response to the incessant suggestions that *Jagged Little Pill* was nothing more than the work of an angry woman venting her spleen. "I think that if you are what you are, people will figure it out," she says. "If they want to see me or anyone as a one-dimensional person then they are missing out on other facets, and that's their choice. Over time, if you listen to the record in its entirety, you will soon come to realize I am not solely an angry person."

But misperceptions couldn't put a dent in *Jagged Little Pill*'s relentless assault on the charts, or in Alanis's popularity. When Grammy time rolled around, the recording industry lavished her with six nominations, tying her with American singer Mariah Carey, whose youthful success and dance-pop stylings were reminiscent of Alanis's early career. "I'm appreciative of this kind of acknowledgement and respect. It feels good to know that my songs have affected people along the way," she said in a written statement issued to the media after the nominations were announced.

On the February 28, 1996, broadcast, she performed a chilling acoustic version of "You Oughta Know," accompanied by a string section, her band, and Glen Ballard on piano. Backstage at the Shrine Auditorium, Ballard said he hoped the quieter, more contemplative rendering of "You Oughta Know" would open people up to reconsider the "angry song." "Hopefully, (listeners) will see a bittersweet, hurt quality. The album version is more angry, but there are other emotions in there," he said.

As they began to hand out the awards, it became evident that the biggest story of the evening would be Alanis, who was called on to make repeated trips to the podium, edging out high-powered competition like Bob Dylan, U2, Nine Inch Nails, Pearl Jam, Tom Petty, and Neil Young. "This is starting to look like a set-up," Canadian record producer David Foster joked at her sweep.

By the end of the evening, she was juggling four Grammys: best album, best rock song, best rock album, and best female rock vocal performance. Each time she made her way to the podium, she conveyed a kind of embarrassment at the honour as well as a latent ambivalence about artistic competition that has lingered since her early *Star Search* appearance. "This award does not represent the fact that I am any better than any of the other women who were nominated with me, but it does represent a lot of people connected to what I wrote," she told the cheering audience when she accepted her best female rock vocal award. She dedicated her album award to "anyone who has ever written . . . from a very spiritual and pure place."

As the cameras panned the star-studded Grammy audience, British singer Annie Lennox was caught leaping to her feet and applauding Alanis wildly. "I think she's absolutely stunning," Lennox said backstage. "She's a rare creature, intensely gifted . . . She looks like someone who can come through and not get wrecked by this business."

Alanis also chose not to go backstage and address the international press horde, which prompted one writer to loudly label her a "spoiled brat." Instead, she wanted to be with the people close to her, who had helped her through the album. Her band, Glen Ballard, Scott Welch, and John Alexander went out for dinner to revel in Alanis's stunning success.

Back home, her parents watched on TV and even they were taken aback by her domination of the awards. "What really surprised us most was album of the year — mostly because nobody was really banking on it," Alan Morissette told the *Ottawa Sun*'s Rick Overall. "When that came up, the whole Morissette entourage went through the roof — a few cheers and a lot of tears. We're so proud of what our daughter has accomplished and frankly as much in awe of her as everyone else. To see that her creativity and music are being appreciated by so many people is just fantastic for the family."

As low-key and underwhelmed as Alanis appeared in victory, Mariah Carey, who was shut out in all six categories, reacted as the "picture of gum-chewing rage," according to *Vanity Fair* magazine. Alanis's victory over Carey was emblematic of the record industry's general turning away from the kind of light pop that had traditionally dominated the Grammys — the kind of music Alanis had made earlier in her career and the kind of music Carey was still selling in platinum quantities. Part of the difference was a change in the way Grammy winners were selected. In recent years, the show had become associated with stodgy, established, safe acts, a trend that reached its nadir the previous year when Tony Bennett and The Three Tenors both managed to land nominations for best album.

To shake things up, instead of having the awards selected by the seven thousand members of the National Association of Recording Arts and Sciences (which organizes the Grammys), their voting was used simply to narrow the selection down to the top twenty vote getters. A panel of "with-it" music industry experts then selected the finalists. The most tangible result of the change in voting was the injection of edgier, younger acts like P. J. Harvey, Pearl Jam, and Alanis.

After the Grammys, her tour picked up again and returned to play Ottawa on March 8. When she arrived home, the mayor presented her with the key to the city and declared it Alanis Morissette Day — on what was already recognized as International Women's Day. "In recognition and celebration of your status as one of this city's great ambassadors to the world, achieved through your critically acclaimed contributions to the popular culture of our times, we celebrate your success and we wish you a lot of luck," Mayor Jackie Holzmann told the singer as they posed for photographs together.

Alanis looked tired and told the press conference she was reluctant to accept a day dedicated to her accomplishments, especially when it fell on a day set aside for all women. She would prefer an Alanis Morissette "moment," so as not to, as she said, "take the spotlight away from my gender. But I accept it in the spirit it was given to me. Which is just sort of a congratulatory thing."

Word leaked out during her return to Ottawa that Alanis was romantically linked to Christian Lane, singer with Loud Lucy, the opening act on her tour. During her set that night at the Congress Centre, she brought Lane out to join her for "Head over Feet" and dedicated the song to "anybody who is currently in love."

Two nights later, Alanis was just outside Toronto at Hamilton's Copps Coliseum for the Juno Awards — the same ceremony that had crowned her most promising female vocalist in 1992. Just like the Grammys, the night belonged to Alanis: album of the year, best rock album, female vocalist of the year, single of the year, and songwriter of the year.

She was introduced by host Anne Murray as "the most honest voice ever to come out of Ottawa" (a jab at her hometown's obsession with politics) and performed a very loose version of "Ironic." "I just want to say that most people have their growth in private. But an artist's is in public. And I thank Canada for accepting that in me," she told the twelve thousand on hand for the ceremony. "It's a pleasure to do what I do and communicate it to you."

Some habits die hard. Even though this was her moment of triumph, her reflex was to downplay her achievements and deflect attention. Having already tasted both cruel rejection and phenomenal acceptance during her career, Alanis was well aware that awards and accolades and money could come and go. What mattered was having the chance to make meaningful music.

17

Perfect

Jesse Tobias strangled a snarling riff from his vintage Fender Jaguar guitar that sent up yet another ecstatic scream from the thirty-five thousand fans at Molson Park in Barrie. The rest of the group kicked in to a version of "You Learn" that was almost unrecognizable from the rendition on *Jagged Little Pill*, signalling the home stretch of the live show.

After wailing the final chorus, Alanis threw down her microphone and made a mad dash across the stage. As her bandmates continued playing, she hammered out some chords on a guitar, leapt on Lashley's back, charged behind the drums to pound out a tribal solo with Hawkins, and then threw her head back and performed a madcap, skipping dance that was awkward and celebratory — like a school kid at recess, desperate to squeeze the last moments of glee from playtime.

A plastic water bottle arched out of the undulating moshpit and sailed near her head. She didn't flinch. Her eyes were locked shut, oblivious to all but the music.

▽

If there's a central irony to the whole Alanis Morissette story, it is this: After a life spent in the public eye, focused on meeting the expectations of others, Alanis has learned to abandon external pressures and to please herself. And the very moment she made that transition, when she learned to get beyond the judgments of others and focus on expressing herself through music, the world learned to love her like never before. "It's the most fulfilling thing. The moment I let go of being motivated by different things is the moment that I got the most adulation," Alanis says.

Hit records come and go, but you could search deep into the music biz almanac and not find a precedent for her success. According to *Rolling Stone*, in the fifty-nine-week period between August 6, 1995, and September 22, 1996, *Jagged Little Pill* sold more than 100,000 copies . . . every week. "Typically, just a handful of records reach that plateau for any given week. To do it for more than a year is virtually unheard of," the magazine reported, adding the album was number one for thirteen weeks and was in the top five for fifty-two of those fifty-nine weeks.

Spin's 1996 year-end issue reported that *Jagged Little Pill*'s sales equalled the combined sales of all twenty albums in *Spin*'s best-of-'96 list. The magazine also calculated that *Jagged Little Pill* had outsold Madonna's *Like a Virgin* and Mariah Carey's *Daydream* by a ratio of 3:2; outsold *Live Through This* by headline-grabbing Courtney Love's band Hole by a ratio of 11:1; and outsold critics' darling Liz Phair's *Exile in Guyville* by 50:1. *Spin* went on to calculate that Alanis outsold all other artists on the Maverick label in 1996 by a ratio of 17:1. The amount of money spent by the public on her records even exceeded campaign spending by presidential candidates Bob Dole and Bill Clinton by 4:3.

During the summer of 1996, the *Los Angeles Times* reported that *Jagged Little Pill* had outsold Hootie and the Blowfish's nine-million-selling debut *Cracked Rear View* and was set to overtake the debut album by the seventies group Boston as bestselling debut album ever (because it was the first of her records to receive international distribution, the U.S. industry was considering *Jagged Little Pill* as Alanis's first). According to the article, Maverick was forecasting worldwide sales of twenty million for *Jagged Little Pill.* Not even competition from superstar acts like REM, Pearl Jam, Counting Crows, Sheryl Crow, and Nirvana's live album could stop the record's relentless march.

Prior to December 1996, U.S. sales were at fourteen million and expected to go much higher with Christmas and then the Grammys in February (where "Ironic" was in the running for record and video of the year but lost in both categories to music legends — Eric Clapton for record of the year and The Beatles for video). Unless U.S. sales dipped severely, the *Times* story suggested *Jagged Little Pill* could go on to outsell *The Bodyguard* soundtrack and Bruce Springsteen's *Born in the USA* (at fifteen million each), *Led Zeppelin IV* (sixteen million), and Fleetwood Mac's *Rumours* (seventeen million). If that happens, it will make *Jagged Little Pill* the third-biggest-selling album in U.S. history, behind Michael Jackson's *Thriller* (at twenty-four million) and The Eagles' *Their Greatest Hits* (at twenty-two million), the *Times* reported.

Not everyone was convinced of *Jagged Little Pill*'s merits, though. No less an authority than sunshine girl singer Debbie Boone, whose immortal 1977 hit, "You Light Up My Life," was sugary enough to cause a diabetic reaction, took the singer to task for her frank language and influence on impressionable kids: "I was angry that middle-of-the-road, Top 40 stations that all kids listen to were playing songs with lyric content like that," the Canadian Press quoted Boone. "At least my 12-year-old twin girls didn't even understand the lyrics that were upsetting me so badly."

And then when "Ironic" was released as a single, language lovers took exception to her description of irony. Editorialists and teachers described most of the scenarios in the song not as true examples of irony, but merely sad coincidences. In the *Washington Post*, writer Richard Leiby scolded her for polluting the song with "a series of events that qualify as annoying or unfortunate, but wouldn't pass for ironic in most freshman English courses." Getting a death-row pardon after the switch has been thrown is simply bad luck; being strapped into the electric chair, winning a reprieve, and then dying of a heart attack — now that would be ironic, he added.

But her purpose in writing "Ironic" was not to provide a textbook definition of the term. It was meant as an expression of her new-found stoic acceptance of whatever delights or miseries life hands out. "It was a journey, a way for me to write fun, stupid, scary, confusing stuff," she says. "The concept of yin and yang, and how when you are in the depths of despair and something really amazing will happen. And then things will be going really great and a wrench will be thrown in."

Miss Thing's reversal of fortune and artistic about-face was viewed with even more skepticism in her homeland. A vocal minority declared that her move from featherweight pop to the unflinching honesty of her new music was nothing more than an opportunistic attempt to cash in on "alternative music."

Further muddying the issue was the fate of her first two MCA albums. Rumours had it that the label — under pressure from Alanis — was destroying existing copies and recalling the records from stores. Then her longtime associate John Alexander was quoted in the *Los Angeles Times*: "We've got a career going here that has nothing to do with those early albums. She doesn't want them on the street here — and neither do we . . . We have a definite thought about what we want to do with those first two albums: Bury them, burn them. We don't want to deal with them." Alexander denies making those comments. And a source at MCA in Canada says the label never recalled the albums but stopped producing the early discs voluntarily. Welch says this was done to avoid exploiting her new fans, who conceivably would buy the old music, anticipating something along the lines of *Jagged Little Pill.*

Music industry cynics weren't the only ones expressing doubts about Alanis. Although she paid homage to Joni Mitchell in her song "Your House" and had reportedly come to adore the Canadian-born singer's work, the admiration was apparently not mutual. When quizzed about her influence on contemporary music by *Details* magazine, Mitchell declared: "I *am* an arrogant artist . . . I get *really* arrogant when they start pitting me against people and saying something or someone's like me when that something is mediocre!"

Mitchell went on to describe Alanis and Sheryl Crow as "made" women and suggested they lean too heavily on their male collaborators. "I'm a musical explorer and not just a pop songwriter or an occasional writer of a song or half a song, like these other women. Alanis Morissette writes words, someone else helps set it to music, and then she's kind of stylized into the part."

In a subsequent December 1, 1996, Mitchell profile in the *New York Times*, writer Stephen Holden reported that Alanis wept after reading Mitchell's criticism, but the younger singer was still being considered to induct Mitchell into the Rock 'n' Roll Hall of Fame in May 1997.

In its 1995 year-end poll, the Toronto-based entertainment magazine *Eye* asked Canadian critics: "Is Alanis Morissette bogus, or what?" The responses were divided, with twenty respondents answering no, and eighteen declaring she was indeed a phoney. The *Toronto Sun*'s Kieran Grant dismissed her as sounding like "a lame hippie." Writer Liisa Ladouceur declared that Alanis "sucks," and blamed the American media for being "out of touch" with "streetwise acts." But writer Karen Bliss wondered why critics were so suspicious of the singer's success. "If I wasn't allowed to change and develop since I was a teenager, I'd still be wearing a purple bandanna around my knee."

Ever since alternative music entered the mainstream, an unstated rule has come into effect in the rock underground: The less you sell, the less you sell out, and the greater your hip cachet. On the other hand, sometimes by the sheer tonnage of records sold, the music can take on a cultural significance that outweighs any critical assessment of the music itself. And so with *Jagged Little Pill*; no matter what anyone thinks of the record itself, the fact that it connected with such a wide audience gave it a significance that could not be denied. When you come from nowhere and put the boots to critical and media favourites like Liz Phair or Hole, or nudge past Boston and elbow aside Whitney Houston . . . well, suddenly, you have to acknowledge that there's more going on than just shrewd promotion. But at the very moment a performer taps into that mysterious connection with the big wide public, the performer also violates the hipster's credo. If your record sells a lot, deep down inside, it *must* suck. Or it must be the result of sinister calculation and nefarious marketing.

When the debate spilled over into cyberspace on music-oriented forums, anonymously posted exchanges were alternately hilarious and vicious. "It just seems too good to be true that she decides to change to this style of music now," one detractor announced. "I'll stop being cynical if she's still playing this form of music in a year or so, and not jumping on some other bandwagon!!"

"Yeah, I fully expect that if gangsta rap makes a big comeback, we'll have Alanis in big jeans telling us about growing up on the mean streets of (the Ottawa suburb) Barrhaven," another netsurfer wrote.

Along with the dozens of web sites devoted to praising her, some naysayers created their own anti-Alanis web site. The attacks prompted this Internet newsgroup response from an American fan: "Why is everybody giving her such a hard time for work she did in her teens? It's as though you really resent the fact that she's trying to do something different now and won't allow her a scrap of credibility."

That argument is echoed by her colleagues. "All the bullshit about her being fabricated. I was there," says Welch. "I was in the studio. I saw what she went through. That's just all crap. That is people taking shots because they don't want to believe . . . The thing that people are really unforgiving about is that you go through a major change in your values, everything, from the time you are sixteen to twenty-one. You move out of the house, you realize everything your parents said wasn't true. People refuse to give her that space." No one can really know how we would react to celebrity at such an early age, he adds. "I think the difference now is, at fourteen, she's got the record company telling her to do something. You can't make all the right decisions. Now, she is making her own decisions."

Ballard, who went through the ordeal of making *Jagged Little Pill*, is disturbed by the public doubts concerning Alanis's genuineness. "It was really, truly the most uncalculated thing that I have ever been involved with. There's no doubt it was a genuine and artistic awakening," he says. "If we had been calculating, we would have looked at what she had done before and said: How can we relate what we are doing now to what you did? I had never even heard that stuff on her first two albums . . . We had our hands on the Ouija board, and it just took off. We were giving blood every time we sat down to do it."

Her former producer, Leslie Howe, says he can especially relate to how the criticism must make Alanis feel. His own band, Sal's Birdland, faced similar criticism in light of Howe's work years ago in the pop group One To One. "People who put labels on things and say this isn't her . . . It makes me mad, actually. Why should she be doing dance pop now? Things have changed, times have changed. She doesn't like to do that kind of music. This is what she likes to do. If you listen to Alanis's lyrics, you know it is not manufactured. This is her."

If she had had the confidence and clout to assert more control over her music earlier in her career, Alanis may well have moved in this musical direction a lot sooner, according to Stephan Klovan. "She had a tendency to be leaning toward that (*Jagged Little Pill* style) all along. It's part of her evolution as a performer. She was held back to a certain degree in her earlier years. Finally she took the bull by the horns and did it."

For her part, Alanis says she expected doubters. If anything, she has been pleased by the acceptance and is philosophical about the criticism, which she does not read. "One minute I'm the best album of the year, the next I'm the worst thing that has ever been created on the earth. So if I want to go on that roller coaster ride, then I am an idiot," she says. A vivid illustration of that roller coaster ride came in *Rolling Stone*'s 1997 readers' poll. *Jagged Little Pill* was selected as worst album and Alanis was voted the second-worst artist of the year, but readers also named her the number-three best artist of the year, behind Smashing Pumpkins and Beck.

Alanis believes the people who truly connect with her music (she calls them "the beautiful spirits") aren't likely to make a point of loudly proclaiming their affection for her. It's the negative people who make all the noise. So she just tunes them out. "Light energy is not very loud. Darkness is very, very loud. I have to keep that in mind and remind myself of that."

Much of her earlier career has been documented, and her recent success has been inescapable. What's missing, what no one was around to see, was the painful process of learning to become a writer and learning to deal with her inner turmoil, she says. So naturally, the change was too abrupt for some. "I know the truth and I think the last time I was seen publicly in Ottawa doing music was a few years ago. And during that time a lot of things happened. There was no one that was walking by my side, documenting all the changes, both personal and creative," she says.

The backlash hurt for "about a month." But she cured herself through meditation and getting "centred" again. And she says she can see why people were cautious about accepting her growth. "If anyone has the incentive and curiosity to find out the truth, they will. And if they don't, I can't control that." If anything, she expected the doubts to be more widespread. "Nothing has really surprised me. I knew people would have a little bit of trepidation towards what I was communicating now, compared to what I was prepared to communicate back then. And so far, a lot of people have been very open to it. Perhaps a little more open than I thought they would be."

▽

As her tour wound down at the end of 1996, Alanis returned to her newly purchased home in Los Angeles and was joined by her family for a calm Christmas. Relations with her family seem to be, if anything, even closer now — especially with her brother Wade, the twin with whom she shared her show business dream so long ago. Recently, after returning from a stay in India, Wade has gone back to performing, gigging around night clubs in his new home, Vancouver.

Friends say that since the tour, Alanis is tired but happier than she has ever been. Some have anticipated that she must be feeling intense pressure to come up with some new music to equal *Jagged Little Pill*. In fact, with the end of her tour, Alanis is relishing her first break from the grind of playing, recording, and writing in close to ten years. "I am so free right now," she laughs. "You know when you would feel the pressure? If you were trying to recreate the external success and I am absolutely not aiming for that," she says.

Alanis is content to wait until she is fully ready to make another record. And she suggests she's prepared to wait a long time. "If I take six months to do this record or seven years or seventy years, it doesn't matter," she says.

During brief breaks from the road, however, she did manage to squeeze in some songwriting with Ballard. "Despite a six-month hiatus, she walks into the studio and, bam! It's back. It is extraordinary," the producer says. The new Ballard collaborations and some compositions with her band were quickly incorporated into the live show: the stomping, spirited "Death of Cinderella" and "King of Intimidation" (which includes a dialogue clip from a 1950 documentary entitled *A Date with Your Family*), "Can't Not" (unabashedly directed at her detractors and built around a slinky riff reminiscent of Led Zeppelin's "Dazed and Confused"), the self-referential band composition "I Don't Know" (which includes lyrical references to each member of her troupe), and the delicate "No Pressure over Cappuccinos." The latter, co-written with Lashley, is among her prettiest songs and when performing the song in concert, she has told audiences it is inspired by Wade. Beyond appearing on the bushels of illicitly recorded bootleg concert CDs that have appeared in the wake of her success, the fate of those new songs is uncertain. "If the time comes and I find I have moved on too far, I would have no qualms about letting them go," Alanis says.

She's open to writing another album with Glen Ballard and says she has "every reason to believe Glen and I will come up with some more magic, but I am not pressuring him or me to come up with that." But she says she would also like to experiment with writing alone and with her band members. "I will never paint myself into a corner," she says. "If I am supposed to be writing this record and it is a part of my path, then I am going to do it. If it is supposed to be drastically different because I change a lot, then it will be. All I know is, whatever music I have put out in my life is an exact snapshot of what my head and my heart were at the time. I have every reason to believe that will never change."

Her most immediate plans involve getting her spiritual life back on track. Meditation and her long-standing interest in psychology are obviously very important to her. "I had to put it a little bit on the back burner, which I will never do again."

Current career plans involve getting back into acting, likely before work even begins on her next record. "Acting plans are as definite as they need to be. Not an actual project I am working on. But I am very open to exploring that part of myself and that part of the art world. But not for the sake of anything other than being excited by what it will require of me. And it will require a lot. I know it," she says.

She also edited together a film of one of her concerts, in New Orleans, for TV (it was shown in Canada in March, 1997). In fact, throughout the tour, she kept a Hi-8 video diary. She has slowly been wading through seventy-eight hours of footage and may eventually edit it together. "It will be a show that will be an hour or two or three long, that I may or may not sell at some point. It will be like a home video," she says. "That is really exciting for me, only in that it allows me to reflect and see how different I have become in the last year and a half."

Whatever she does next, her manager Scott Welch believes the bond she has forged with her fans will be a lasting one. "I can always tell by looking at fan mail. Other clients, who I don't want to name, they want your picture, they want it autographed," he says. "Her fan mail is: 'Hey I was really down in the dumps. Your song got me through' . . . They never ask for things. That's a sense that people are bonding with her in a way that is emotional as well as musical."

Such an intimate bond with her fans has created a fervour for details about her life. Even her devoted fans are susceptible to wild rumours and innuendo. Internet sites have been filled with crazy stories that had Alanis OD-ing on drugs or hospitalized with exhaustion or poised to make unlikely disclosures about her sexual orientation. There have been "revelations" that she didn't actually write the songs on *Jagged Little Pill*, and others that claim she ghost-wrote material for the Spice Girls. It seems the more outrageous the suggestion, the more likely it is to gain currency.

But the most consistent claim about Alanis Morissette is that she can't hope to equal the commercial triumph of *Jagged Little Pill*, that she will fold under the pressure of following up such an enormous success. It's true that the record's achievement will be difficult to match, but is following up a mega-platinum album any more stressful than some of the things she has already been through?

Alanis has already been dismissed as a has-been once in her career, and she went on to unfathomable success. But if *Jagged Little Pill* was the culmination of a lifetime spent being groomed for pop stardom, striving for excellence, concealing doubts and frustrations, stifling anger, enduring emotional upheaval and condescending judgments, learning to trust instincts, and surviving success, what's left for her to write about? Not to worry, says Alanis.

"This is the first time in my life I have ever been still," she says. "A lot of things I have repressed are coming out now, and there are tons of them."

Jagged Little Pill really is just the beginning, she adds. "In many ways, I really feel that I have only scratched the surface. I know there are a million more revelations and thoughts and confusions that I haven't even begun to write about yet."

Appendix 1

DJ Surveys

The following two surveys show the generally stellar ratings DJs gave Alanis's first record, "Fate Stay with Me." The surveys were conducted by a Kentucky-based record pool, which distributes records to nightclub DJs. (The surveys were provided courtesy of Louis Gaspar.)

PRODUCT FEEDBACK REPORT

KYOHVA RECORD POOL
2240 CENTRAL AVENUE
ASHLAND, KY 41101-7842
606-329-1851

ROGER E. HILLMAN
Director

LOUIS. M. GASPAR
Executive Director

DATA BOX

DATE RECEIVED	17 April 1987
FEEDBACK DATE	13 May 1987
SERVICED BY	MPL Promotions

OVERALL POOL AVERAGES
DJ OPINION — 5.
AUDIENCE RESPONSE — 4.33

Artist __Alanis Morisette__
Title __Fate Stay With Me__
Label __Lamour Records__
Stock # __LMR-10-12__
Format __7"__
Quantity Serviced __3__

SERVICED BIN NUMBER

RATING EVALUATION

5 Excellent
4 Very Good
3 Good
2 Fair
1 Poor
0 Non-Programmed

MEMBER	DJ OPINION	AUDIENCE RESPONSE	DANCEABILITY	MIXABILITY	VOCAL	INSTRUMENTS	CLUB POTENTIAL	RADIO POTENTIAL	DJ COMMENTS
1 ROGER E. HILLMAN, Director	5	4	5	3	5	5	5	5	Both A & B ati
2 LOUIS M. GASPAR, Executive Director	5	5	5	4	5	4	5	5	Fate Stay
3 Marvin Collett									
4 Steve Smallwood, Billboard Reporter									
5 Richard B. McDonald									

PRODUCT FEEDBACK REPORT

KYOHVA RECORD POOL
2240 CENTRAL AVENUE
ASHLAND, KY 41101-7842
606-329-1851

ROGER E. HILLMAN
Director

LOUIS. M. GASPAR
Executive Director

DATA BOX

DATE RECEIVED	18 May 1987
FEEDBACK DATE	03 June 1987
SERVICED BY	MPL Promotions

1" Wow!

OVERALL POOL AVERAGES
DJ OPINION — 3.10
AUDIENCE RESPONSE — 2.70

Artist __Alanis Morissette__
Title __Fate Stay With Me/Find The Right Man__
Label __Lamor Records__
Stock # __LMR-10-12__
Format __7"__
Quantity Serviced __10__

SERVICED BIN NUMBER

RATING EVALUATION

5 Excellent
4 Very Good
3 Good
2 Fair
1 Poor
0 Non-Programmed

MEMBER	DJ OPINION	AUDIENCE RESPONSE	DANCEABILITY	MIXABILITY	VOCAL	INSTRUMENTS	CLUB POTENTIAL	RADIO POTENTIAL	DJ COMMENTS
1 ROGER E. HILLMAN, Director	4	4	4	4	5	4	4	4	
2 LOUIS M. GASPAR, Executive Director									
3 Marvin Collett	½	3	½	2	3	3	3	3	
4 Steve Smallwood, Billboard Reporter	3	3	3	3	3	3	3	3	
5 Richard B. McDonald									
6 Bob Sussman	3	½	2	3	3	3	2	2	
7 Tim A. Mason									
8 Walt Barner									
9 Burnett Dotson	3	3	3	2	4	4	3	2	
10 Martin D. Achtermann									
11 E. Wayne Flynn									
12 Jay Lamka	2	2	2	2	2	2	2	2	How about a 12?
13 Scott Langer	1	0	1	1	1	1	1	1	when it's on 12 call me
14 Don Walker									
15 W.A.C.									
16 William Kitter	4	2	4	4	5	5	3	1	
17 Paul Main									
18 Jerry Fletcher	3	3	3	2	4	4	4	2	
19 G. Keith Jarrell	4	4	5	3	5	5	5	3	12" PLEASE
20 Walter B. Wright, Jr.									
21 Thom S. Smith									
22 John Sutter									
23 Randy Justice									
24 Chuck Horn									
25 Tony T. Field									

Appendix 2

Postcard from the Junos

I n 1992, when Alanis was nominated for three Juno Awards (Canada's equivalent of the Grammys), she prepared a special "postcard from the Junos," detailing the experience of attending the awards for publication in the *Ottawa Sun*. She dictated the column to the *Sun*'s Rick Overall prior to winning the award for most promising female vocalist. The text appears below.

JUNO POSTCARD

(*Sun*) Editor's Note — In her March 1992 postcard from the Junos, Ottawa's pop princess Alanis fills us in on the craziness surrounding the buildup for Canada's BIG music weekend. With nominations in three categories — single of the year, most promising female vocalist and best dance recording — it's looking pretty positive for our gal. Even though it's a nerve-wracking time, she consented to give us a peek from inside the Juno madhouse. But for now, all Ottawa's got their fingers crossed — good luck, Alanis!

APPENDIX 2

TORONTO — Talk about nerves!

It's Juno weekend and my dreams are coming true. After all the work, there's a chance I might just be rewarded with a Juno tonight — but let's not talk about that, we don't want to jinx things, do we?

They said this was a high-pressure time for nominees, and they weren't fooling. On Thursday, I spent a lot of time doing phone interviews with writers from across the country — and wrapped it up with an hour on one of TO's top dance shows.

But, that's just the beginning!

Yesterday, things started to get really wild. I spent some time taking in the seminars and lectures at "The Record" conference which brings together music retailers, musicians, entertainment professionals (lawyers, agents and managers) and music journalists.

Everybody talks shop, so I just figured I'd check it out and maybe pick up a tip or two.

In the middle of that we dashed around the city — putting in appearances at MuchMusic and on "Electric Circus."

And last night I got to have a little fun at Rock 'n' Bowl — the industry's big celebrity bowling challenge out in Scarborough.

But we had to cut the fun short, because this morning I was up bright and early and looking at a pretty heavy schedule, with the bulk of it devoted to rehearsing for the big show tonight. In fact, rehearsal starts at 9 a.m.

Then it's back to the hotel to change into my special Juno outfit. I know for a fact that no other girl will be wearing it, because I helped design the outfit with a friend — so I think I'm safe from copycats.

It looks like we'll be busy all afternoon. There's a pre-show bash at the O'Keefe Centre, a meet-the-nominees reception and another pre-show function where they'll hand out a lot of the Junos which aren't presented on the actual show. Some of my categories fall into this area, so I'll be nervous all afternoon.

When it's showtime, they've actually got me pegged to present a Juno — but I don't know for what. I'm just worried about flubbing my lines. I guess if I just pretend the whole thing is no big deal I won't get nervous.

Who am I kidding?

This is the biggest deal ever.

Appendix 3

Songs

Here's an incomplete list of known Alanis Morissette compositions, both recorded and unreleased. Collaborators, when known, are mentioned in brackets (* denotes a commercially unavailable or unrecorded song).

Fate Stay with Me
Find the Right Man (also listed in publishing records as You Found the
    Right Man)
* I Gotta Go
* Another Sleepless Night (with Lindsay Morgan)
* Your Dream Has Come in Time
* Over Now
* Get with It
* Toughen Up

* This Feeling
* Be There as My Friend
Feel Your Love (with Leslie Howe)
Too Hot (with Leslie Howe)
Plastic (with Leslie Howe and Serge Côté)
Walk Away (with Leslie Howe, Frank Levin, and Louise Reny)
On My Own (with Leslie Howe and Serge Côté)
Superman (with Leslie Howe)
Jealous (with Leslie Howe and Serge Côté)
Human Touch (with Frank Levin, Louise Reny, and Leslie Howe)
Oh Yeah (with Leslie Howe)
Party Boy (with Leslie Howe)
Real World (with Leslie Howe and Serge Côté)
An Emotion Away (with Leslie Howe and Serge Côté)
Rain (with Leslie Howe and Serge Côté)
The Time of Your Life (with Leslie Howe and Serge Côté)
No Apologies (with Leslie Howe and Serge Côté)
Can't Deny (with Leslie Howe and Serge Côté)
When We Meet Again (with Leslie Howe and Serge Côté)
Give What You Got (with Leslie Howe and Serge Côté)
(Change Is) Never a Waste of Time (with Leslie Howe and Serge Côté)
Big Bad Love (with Leslie Howe and Serge Côté)
* I Wantcha (with Leslie Howe and Serge Côté)
* Gone (with Steve Haflidson)
* Taking Back the Night (with Steve Haflidson)
* If I Should Be with You (with Steve Haflidson)
* Angel of Mercy (with Anthony Vanderburgh)
* Spectrum of Color (with Anthony Vanderburgh)
* Believe Again (with Anthony Vanderburgh)
* Anyway (with David Charles Pickell)
* Come Into Her Own (with Dean McTaggart)
* Comfort (with Terry Sawchuk, credited as Terrence Lee)
* Fading (with Paul Howard Gordon)
* Souvenirs (with Amy Sky)
* Last Time (with Daniel Leblanc)

* My Cathedral (with Paul Howard Gordon and Tom P. Keane)
* My Last Tear (with David Baxter)
* Talk to Your Heart (with David Baxter)
* That'd Be Nice (with David Baxter)
* One Thing I Forgot (with Edward Sydney Schwartz)
* Stay with Me (with Regina Schock)
* Taste My Spirit (with Rick Neigher)
* Used to Run (with Tim Thorney)
* Bottom Line (with Glen Ballard)
* Closer than You Might Believe (with Glen Ballard)
* Keep the Radio On (with Glen Ballard)
* No Avalon (with Glen Ballard)
* Superstar Wonderful Weirdos (with Glen Ballard and Terry Sawchuk, credited as Terrence Lee)
* Why Can't I (with Glen Ballard)
All I Really Want (with Glen Ballard)
You Oughta Know (with Glen Ballard)
Perfect (with Glen Ballard)
Hand in My Pocket (with Glen Ballard)
Right Through You (with Glen Ballard, also published as Right Thru You)
Forgiven (with Glen Ballard)
You Learn (with Glen Ballard)
Head over Feet (with Glen Ballard)
Mary Jane (with Glen Ballard)
Ironic (with Glen Ballard)
Not the Doctor (with Glen Ballard)
Wake Up (with Glen Ballard)
* Death of Cinderella (with Glen Ballard)
* King of Intimidation (with Glen Ballard)
* No Pressure over Cappuccinos (with Nick Lashley)
* I Don't Know (with Nick Lashley, Chris Chaney, Taylor Hawkins, and Jesse Tobias)
* Can't Not

Appendix 4

Tour Dates

The following is a detailed list of the tour dates Alanis and her band performed in support of *Jagged Little Pill*. Some early performances in Los Angeles and the June 20, 1996 showcase at Zaphod Beeblebrox are not included in the list. (The dates are provided courtesy of POLLSTAR, The Concert Hotwire.)

07/11/95	Tempe	AZ	Electric Ballroom
07/14/95	San Jose	CA	Cactus Club
07/15/95	San Francisco	CA	Bottom of the Hill
07/17/95	Portland	OR	Berbati's Pan
07/18/95	Seattle	WA	Weathered Walk
07/19/95	Vancouver	BC	Starfish Room
07/22/95	Denver	CO	Mercury Cafe
07/24/95	Minneapolis	MN	Fine Line Music Cafe

07/25/95	Milwaukee	WI	Shank Hall
07/26/95	Chicago	IL	Metro
07/28/95	Indianapolis	IN	Patio
07/29/95	Pontiac	MI	7th House
07/31/95	Cleveland	OH	Grog Shop
08/01/95	Toronto	ONT	Lee's Palace
08/10/95	Montreal	QUE	Cafe Campus
08/11/95	Providence	RI	Club Babyhead
08/13/95	Boston	MA	Paradise Rock Club
08/16/95	New York	NY	Tramps
08/17/95	Philadelphia	PA	Theatre of Living Arts
08/19/95	Washington	DC	9:30 Club
08/20/95	Cleveland	OH	Odeon Concert Club
08/22/95	Atlanta	GA	Masquerade
08/23/95	Nashville	TN	328 Performance Hall
08/24/95	Memphis	TN	New Daisy Theater
08/26/95	New Orleans	LA	Howlin' Wolf
08/27/95	Houston	TX	Numbers
08/29/95	Austin	TX	Liberty Lunch
08/30/95	Dallas	TX	Trees
09/01/95	Columbia	MO	Blue Note
09/02/95	Cincinnati	OH	Bogart's
09/07/95	New York	NY	MTV Awards
09/09/95	Cuyahoga Falls	OH	Blossom Music Center
09/14/95	Las Vegas	NV	Palladium
09/17/95	Los Angeles	CA	John Anson Ford Theater
09/18/95	Los Angeles	CA	John Anson Ford Theater
09/25/95	Helsinki	FIN	MuchMusic Awards
09/26/95	Helsinki	FIN	MuchMusic Awards
09/29/95	London	UK	Subterania
10/03/95	Madrid	SPA	El Sol
10/06/95	Vienna	AUT	Szene Wien
10/07/95	Vienna	AUT	Szene Wien
10/08/95	Frankfurt	GER	Nachtleben
10/10/95	Berlin	GER	Loft
10/11/95	Hamburg	GER	Markthalle
10/13/95	Baden Baden	GER	SWF 3 Radio
10/15/95	Cologne	GER	Kantine
10/17/95	Amsterdam	NET	Milky Way

APPENDIX 4

10/18/95	Paris	FRA	Erotika Club
10/19/95	Paris	FRA	Erotika Club
10/20/95	Glasgow	UK	Garage
10/22/95	Manchester	UK	Manchester University
10/23/95	London	UK	Shepherd's Bush Empire
10/28/95	New York	NY	Saturday Night Live
10/31/95	Osaka	JAP	IMP Hall
11/02/95	Nagoya	JAP	Club Quattro
11/04/95	Tokyo	JAP	Ebisu Garden Hall
11/05/95	Tokyo	JAP	Ebisu Garden Hall
11/14/95	Santa Barbara	CA	Arlington Theater
11/15/95	San Francisco	CA	Warfield Theater
11/17/95	Seattle	WA	Paramount Theater
11/18/95	Salem	OR	Salem Armory
11/20/95	Salt Lake City	UT	State Fair Coliseum
11/22/95	Denver	CO	Paramount Theater
11/24/95	Omaha	NE	Mancuso Hall
11/25/95	Davenport	IA	Adler Theater
11/26/95	Indianapolis	IN	Egyptian Room
11/28/95	Toronto	ONT	Warehouse
11/29/95	Montreal	QUE	Metropolis
12/01/95	Newark	DE	Bob Carpenter Center
12/02/95	Alfred	NY	McLain Center
12/04/95	University Park	PA	Pennsylvania St. Univ.
12/05/95	Wilkes-Barre	PA	Marts Center
12/06/95	Geneseo	NY	Kuhl Hall
12/12/95	Detroit	MI	State Theater
01/03/96	La Jolla	CA	Rimac Arena
01/04/96	Irvine	CA	Crawford Hall
01/04/96	Irvine	CA	Crawford Hall
01/06/96	Mesa	AZ	Mesa Amphitheater
01/06/96	Mesa	AZ	Mesa Amphitheater
01/09/96	Austin	TX	Music Hall
01/10/96	San Antonio	TX	Municipal Auditorium
01/12/96	Dallas	TX	Music Complex
01/13/96	Houston	TX	International Ballroom
01/14/96	New Orleans	LA	UNO Lakefront Arena
01/14/96	New Orleans	LA	UNO Lakefront Arena
01/16/96	Memphis	TN	Auditorium North Hall

01/18/96	Jacksonville	FL	Univ. of No. Florida
01/19/96	Orlando	FL	Bob Carr P.A.C.
01/20/96	Sunrise	FL	Sunrise Music Theater
01/23/96	Atlanta	GA	Fox Theater
01/23/96	Atlanta	GA	Fox Theater
01/24/96	Nashville	TN	Vanderbilt University
01/24/96	Nashville	TN	Vanderbilt University
01/26/96	Charleston	SC	King Street Palace
01/26/96	Charleston	SC	King Street Palace
01/27/96	Raleigh	NC	Raleigh Civic Center
01/29/96	Fairfax	VA	Patriot Center
01/29/96	Fairfax	VA	Patriot Center
01/30/96	Baltimore	MD	UMBC Fieldhouse
02/01/96	Philadelphia	PA	Electric Factory
02/02/96	Pittsburgh	PA	Kennedy Arena
02/04/96	Amherst	MA	Mullins Center
02/06/96	New York	NY	Roseland
02/06/96	New York	NY	Roseland
02/07/96	New York	NY	Roseland
02/07/96	New York	NY	Roseland
02/08/96	New York	NY	Roseland
02/08/96	New York	NY	Roseland
02/10/96	Boston	MA	Gosman Center
02/11/96	Providence	RI	Strand Theater
02/12/96	Durham	NH	Univ. of New Hampshire
02/12/96	Durham	NH	Univ. of New Hampshire
02/13/96	Troy	NY	RPI Fieldhouse
03/26/96	Paris	FRA	La Bataclan
03/28/96	Neu-Isenburg	GER	Hugenottenhalle
03/29/96	Barcelona	SPA	Zeleste
03/31/96	Madrid	SPA	La Riviera
04/02/96	Milan	ITA	Propaganda
04/04/96	Ludwigsburg	GER	Scala Theatre
04/07/96	Brussels	BEL	Lunatheater
04/08/96	Utrecht	NET	Music Centre
04/09/96	Hamburg	GER	Markthalle
04/11/96	Stockholm	SWE	Cirkus
04/12/96	Copenhagen	DEN	Grey Hall
04/14/96	London	UK	Shepherd's Bush Empire

04/15/96	London	UK	Shepherd's Bush Empire
04/16/96	London	UK	Shepherd's Bush Empire
04/18/96	Birmingham	UK	Aston Villa Centre
04/19/96	Manchester	UK	Apollo Manchester
04/20/96	Glasgow	UK	Barrowlands
04/22/96	Dublin	IRE	SFX Centre
04/25/96	Perth	AUS	Metropolis Nightclub
04/28/96	Melbourne	AUS	Palais Theatre
04/30/96	Sydney	AUS	Enmore Theatre
05/01/96	Sydney	AUS	Enmore Theatre
05/02/96	Sydney	AUS	Enmore Theatre
05/04/96	Canberra	AUS	Royal Theatre
05/05/96	Brisbane	AUS	Festival Hall
05/07/96	Wellington	NZ	St. James Theatre
05/08/96	Auckland	NZ	Logan Campbell Theatre
05/31/96	Portland	OR	Rose Garden Arena
06/01/96	George	WA	Gorge
06/03/96	Salt Lake City	UT	Delta Center
06/05/96	Morrison	CO	Red Rocks Amphitheater
06/07/96	Berkeley	CA	Greek Theater
06/08/96	Berkeley	CA	Greek Theater
06/09/96	Sacramento	CA	Cal Expo Amphitheater
06/12/96	Santa Barbara	CA	Santa Barbara Bowl
06/13/96	Las Vegas	NV	Aladdin Theater
06/15/96	Los Angeles	CA	Greek Theater
06/16/96	Los Angeles	CA	Greek Theater
06/18/96	Los Angeles	CA	Greek Theater
06/19/96	Los Angeles	CA	Greek Theater
06/20/96	Irvine	CA	Irvine Meadows Amph.
06/22/96	Del Mar	CA	Del Mar Fairgrounds
06/23/96	Phoenix	AZ	America West Arena
06/25/96	Mexico City	MEX	Metropolitan Theater
06/27/96	Milwaukee	WI	Marcus Amphitheater
06/29/96	London	UK	Hyde Park
07/03/96	Rotterdam	NET	Ahoy
07/04/96	Paris	FRA	Palais Omnisports
07/06/96	Torhout	BEL	Torhout Festival
07/07/96	Werchter	BEL	Werchter Festival
07/09/96	Berlin	GER	Waldbuhne

07/10/96	Leipzig	GER	Festival
07/14/96	Dublin	IRE	Feile
07/16/96	Lyon	FRA	Vienne Festival
07/19/96	Long Marston	UK	Phoenix Festival
07/31/96	Vancouver	BC	General Motors Place
08/02/96	Calgary	ALB	Saddledome
08/03/96	Edmonton	ALB	Edmonton Coliseum
08/05/96	Winnipeg	MAN	Winnipeg Arena
08/08/96	Montreal	QUE	Molson Centre
08/09/96	Ottawa	ONT	Corel Centre
08/10/96	Barrie	ONT	Molson Park
08/12/96	Darien Center	NY	Darien Lake P.A.C.
08/13/96	Mansfield	MA	Great Woods Center
08/14/96	Mansfield	MA	Great Woods Center
08/16/96	Wantagh	NY	Jones Beach Amph.
08/17/96	Wantagh	NY	Jones Beach Amph.
08/19/96	East Rutherford	NJ	Meadowlands Arena
08/20/96	Hartford	CT	Meadows Music Theater
08/22/96	Columbia	MD	Merriweather Post
08/23/96	Philadelphia	PA	CoreStates Spectrum
08/24/96	Bristow	VA	Nissan Pavilion
08/26/96	Hershey	PA	Hersheypark Stadium
08/27/96	Burgettstown	PA	Star Lake Amphitheater
08/29/96	Clarkston	MI	Pine Knob Music Theater
08/31/96	Minneapolis	MN	Target Center
09/01/96	Tinley Park	IL	World Music Theater
09/02/96	Columbus	OH	Polaris Amphitheater
09/06/96	Noblesville	IN	Deer Creek Music Center
09/07/96	Cuyahoga Falls	OH	Blossom Music Center
09/08/96	Cincinnati	OH	Riverbend Music Center
09/10/96	Charlotte	NC	Blockbuster Pavilion
09/11/96	Columbia	SC	Carolina Coliseum
09/13/96	Atlanta	GA	Chastain Park Amph.
09/14/96	Atlanta	GA	Omni
09/15/96	Antioch	TN	Starwood Amphitheater
09/17/96	Knoxville	TN	Thompson-Boling Arena
09/18/96	Raleigh	NC	Walnut Creek Amph.
09/20/96	W. Palm Beach	FL	Coral Sky Amphitheater
09/21/96	St. Petersburg	FL	ThunderDome

09/23/96	Lafayette	LA	Cajundome
09/24/96	Memphis	TN	Pyramid
09/25/96	Maryland Hgts.	MO	Riverport Amphitheater
09/27/96	Dallas	TX	Starplex Amphitheater
09/28/96	Austin	TX	Southpark Meadows
09/29/96	Houston	TX	Summit
10/02/96	New Orleans	LA	UNO Lakefront Arena
10/03/96	New Orleans	LA	UNO Lakefront Arena
10/15/96	Mexico City	MEX	Auditorio Nacional
10/16/96	Mexico City	MEX	Auditorio Nacional
10/21/96	Sao Paulo	BRA	Olympia
10/22/96	Sao Paulo	BRA	Olympia
10/23/96	Rio de Janeiro	BRA	Metropolitan
10/26/96	Buenos Aires	ARG	Obras Sanitarias
10/27/96	Buenos Aires	ARG	Obras Sanitarias
10/29/96	Santiago	CHI	Teatro Monumental
11/11/96	Tokyo	JAP	Alaska Blitz
11/12/96	Tokyo	JAP	Shibuya Kokaido
11/13/96	Tokyo	JAP	NHK Hall
11/15/96	Osaka	JAP	Kouseinenkaikan Hall
11/17/96	Fukuoka	JAP	Shi Min Kaikan
11/19/96	Nagoya	JAP	Century Hall
11/21/96	Seoul	SKO	Sejong Cultural Centre
11/23/96	Manila	PHI	Araneta Coliseum
11/25/96	Taipei	TAI	TICC Hall
11/27/96	Hong Kong	HK	Queen Elizabeth Stadium
11/29/96	Kuala Lumpur	MAL	Stadium Negara
12/01/96	Jakarta	IND	Plenary Hall
12/02/96	Singapore	SIN	Harbour Pavilion
12/04/96	Melbourne	AUS	Flinders Park
12/05/96	Adelaide	AUS	Entertainment Centre
12/06/96	Sydney	AUS	Entertainment Centre
12/08/96	Sydney	AUS	Entertainment Centre
12/10/96	Melbourne	AUS	Flinders Park
12/11/96	Melbourne	AUS	Flinders Park
12/13/96	Auckland	NZ	Mt. Smart Supertop
12/14/96	Honolulu	HI	Richardson Field

Appendix 5

Hospitality Rider

Curious about what it took to feed Alanis and her band and crew on the road? Here's the "hospitality rider" from a late-winter 1996 tour date.

LOAD-IN BREAKFAST (8:30-9 A.M.)
freshly brewed coffee, tea, cream, and sugar
one case assorted soft drinks
twelve bottles of Evian water
1 1/2 dozen bagels, cream cheese, and butter
cereal (Raisin Bran, Rice Crispies, Corn Flakes)
Quaker Instant Oatmeal
grapefruit, melons, and bananas
one gallon milk (and skim milk)
one toaster
four litres orange juice

APPENDIX 5

BUS AND TRUCK DRIVER BREAKFASTS
Three complete HOT breakfasts (eggs, bacon, hash browns, pancakes, and toast) to be delivered by 9 a.m.

CREW LUNCH (1 P.M.)
To serve twelve
Homemade soup or chili with one of the following:
– deli platter of fresh turkey, chicken, salami, ham, roast beef
– charcoal broiled hamburgers, veggie burgers, hot dogs, or grilled chicken breasts
– fresh, sliced cheese
– lettuce, tomato, and appropriate condiments
– two loaves of whole wheat bread, buns
– tuna salad and tossed salad
– sodas, water, coffee, and milk

BAND AND CREW CATERED DINNER (5 P.M.)
Snack trays for both band dressing rooms
– one small deli tray (turkey, chicken, roast beef, cheese, lettuce, tomato, mustard, and mayo), wheat bread
– one vegetable relish tray with dip

DRESSING ROOM ONE (FOR ALANIS MORISSETTE)
Should be clean and set up by 3 p.m., with at least one couch and chairs for six people. Dressing room should have a private toilet, shower where possible, and mirrors.

Food:
Fresh fruit (bananas, apples, oranges, grapes, etc.)
one quart fresh squeezed orange juice
four bottles Gatorade
six Dannon yogurts with fruit
one bag corn chips with salsa
one electric kettle
one box Throat Coat tea
six 1.5 litre Evian bottles
fresh ice for drinks
bottle opener
ten large plastic Solo cups
ceramic coffee mugs

candles
novelties (anything that would make her feel at home)

DRESSING ROOM TWO (FOR BAND)
Should be clean and set up by 3 p.m., with at least one couch and chairs
for ten people. Dressing room should have a private toilet, shower where
possible, and mirrors.

Food:
fresh fruit (bananas, oranges, grapes)
one case imported beer (Heineken, Corona, etc.)
six light beers (Bud Light, etc.)
fourteen 1.5 litre bottles of Evian water
twelve assorted sodas
1/2 gallon fresh squeezed orange juice
1/2 gallon cranberry juice
ten bottles Gatorade
ten assorted candy bars
ceramic coffee mugs
two dozen large Solo plastic cups
one bottle of liquor or wine, to be determined by tour or production
    manager on day of show
four dozen large towels
two bars soap

FOR THE CREW BUS
one case imported or local micro-brewed beer
one case Evian water
one case assorted sodas (Classic Coke, Diet Coke, 7-Up)
one gallon orange juice
one quart of whole milk
one bag potato chips
one bag pretzels
one bag chocolate chip cookies
one bag corn chips, salsa
one jar crunchy peanut butter
one jar strawberry jelly
one loaf whole wheat bread
one bottle chardonnay wine

APPENDIX 5

FOR THE BAND BUS
one case imported or local micro-brewed beer
six light beers
one case Evian water
twelve assorted sodas
1/2 gallon orange juice
one bag potato chips
one bag chocolate chip cookies
one bag corn chips, salsa
one 15-pound bag of ice for each bus
veggie burritos, tacos, sandwiches, pizzas

Index

INDEX

INDEX

Date Due

JUN 16 '97	JUL 1 6 2016	
JUL 7 '97	MAR - 3 2017	
JUL 15 '97	JAN 1 7 2019	
AUG 13 '97		
SEP 23 '97		
APR 1 4 1998		
MAY 1 1 1998		
JUN 2 4 1998		
JAN 31 '02		
JUL 02 '02		
OCT 8 2004		
APR 2 2 2009		
JAN 1 3 2011		
FEB 1 8 2015		
JUL 1 3 2015		